HEY, CAN WE JUST CHILL?

7 EXPLOSIVE STEPS TO PUNCHING ANXIETY IN THE FACE AND REMAINING CALM DURING UNCERTAINTY

SUJITH K. THOMAS

© Copyright 2021 - All rights reserved.

The content contained within this book may not be reproduced, duplicated, or transmitted without direct written permission from the author or the publisher.

Under no circumstances will any blame or legal responsibility be held against the publisher, or author, for any damages, reparation, or monetary loss due to the information contained within this book, either directly or indirectly.

Identifiers: ISBN 978-1-7777012-0-8 (paperback) | ISBN 978-1-7777012-1-5 (hardcover) | ISBN 978-1-7777012-2-2 (eBook) | 978-1-7777012-3-9 (audiobook)

Legal Notice:

This book is copyright protected. It is only for personal use. You cannot amend, distribute, sell, use, quote, or paraphrase any part, or the content within this book, without the consent of the author or publisher.

Disclaimer Notice:

Please note the information contained within this document is for educational and entertainment purposes only. All effort has been executed to present accurate, up-to-date, reliable, complete information. No warranties of any kind are declared or implied. Readers acknowledge that the author is not engaged in the rendering of legal, financial, medical, or professional advice. The content within this book has been derived from various sources. Please consult a licensed professional before attempting any techniques outlined in this book.

By reading this document, the reader agrees that under no circumstances is the author responsible for any losses, direct or indirect, that are incurred as a result of the use of the information contained within this document, including, but not limited to, errors, omissions, or inaccuracies.

CONTENTS

PART ONE

WHY I CREATED THE 7 EXPLOSIVE STEPS   2

KNOWING YOUR ENEMY IN THE BATTLEFIELD   11

1. It's More Than Just Worrying
2. Stress vs. Anxiety vs. Depression
3. Anxiety Medication: Take It or Leave It?

PART TWO

EXPLOSIVE STEP #1   36

DECODING AND NAMING YOUR STORM

4. It's Okay To Freak Out!
5. Identifying Anxiety Triggers
6. Mindfully Sitting With Your Anxiety

EXPLOSIVE STEP #2   65

QUADRUPLING YOUR GRATITUDE

7. The Science of Gratitude
8. The Secret Virtue to Developing a Grateful Heart
9. The Power of Positive Repetition

EXPLOSIVE STEP #3   93

SMASHING OUTLIER EVENTS

10. When An Outlier Isn't Cool
11. Overthinking and the Fear of Failure

EXPLOSIVE STEP #4   130

KICKSTARTING A MEANINGFUL LIFE

12. Don't Be Bothered With What People Think of You
13. Forgive Yourself for Your Past Mistakes
14. Build a Strong Support System

EXPLOSIVE STEP #5   160

INTENSIFYING WORKOUTS WITH BRAIN FOOD

15. The Connection Between Mental Health and Working Out
16. Load up on Brain Food
17. Three Harmful Eating Habits to Break Now

EXPLOSIVE STEP #6   183

TRIGGERING THE LAST CHORE

18. How Anxious People Feel About Bedtime
19. How to Beat Night-time Anxiety and Reclaim Your Beauty Sleep

EXPLOSIVE STEP #7   198

BEING PROACTIVE WITH COMMITMENTS

20. Creating an Action Plan to Deal With Your Anxiety

CONCLUSION   208

REFERENCES   213

PART 1

INTRODUCTION

WHY I CREATED THE 7 EXPLOSIVE STEPS

If you knew me back in 2006, you'd see a regular teenage boy with an acne-spotted face—acne so bad that one of my high school teachers felt the need to ask if I was struggling with a case of chickenpox. On top of this, I received a lot of pressure from my family to excel at school.

Already, I had two emotional battles I was struggling with: the insecurity about my physical appearance because of my spotted face, and my tendency to be a people pleaser so I could meet everybody else's expectations of me. That's enough emotional turmoil to drive anyone, regardless of their age, into a state of chronic stress and anxiety.

How I dealt with these pressures didn't make things any better. I developed compulsive behaviors that would bring me a sense of comfort and provide an escape from my current reality. One habit I developed was biting my nails. I could go for hours, not realizing I was chewing past the point of no return. I would also retreat to my bedroom whenever I felt tears welling up in my eyes, and return to my family after my tears had dried up as if nothing had happened.

I became a master at faking my happiness, so good that nobody ever noticed how lonely and afraid I felt inside. I guess a part of me felt as though if people saw my inner cry for help, they would find me less relatable or "cool" to be around. In a way, I also resented myself for having such strong unresolved feelings that were triggered by even the slightest of situations. I would frequently ask myself, "What's wrong with you? Why are you so sensitive?"

The truth is, I was battling with depression and anxiety; however, I was never diagnosed with it. Nobody around me had ever been diagnosed with mental illness, and so no one knew what mental illness looked like or how to treat it. Some children at school noticed I was different from the other kids, but to them, being different was like choosing to be an outcast. They bullied me at every opportunity they could find, making sure they highlighted my visible insecurities, as though I wasn't aware of them.

It was only when I left school and became an adult that I realized how normal it was to suffer from anxiety. A certain amount of anxiety is good for you. For instance, if you are anxious right before a presentation, the increase in adrenaline can help you remain alert and on top of your game during the presentation. Feeling anxious before meeting new people is also good. It shows a natural willingness to be liked or accepted, which is part of our basic human instinct.

However, not all anxiety is good, and perhaps this is why it's so difficult to diagnose the condition. The unhealthy kind of anxiety creeps up on you at any moment of the day. You don't have to be doing anything to feel a sudden clump in your chest and an acceleration in your heartbeat. This kind of anxiety is triggered by your thoughts. What's surprising is they don't even need to be thoughts related to what you're doing. You could feel anxious after recalling a painful experience that left you in tatters or thinking about future scenarios which seem too overwhelming to endure.

The unhealthy kind of anxiety triggers the same stress response your brain produces when you are in physical danger. Imagine this for a moment: After having a morbid thought which triggers anxiety, your brain responds as though you were physically threatened. First, this should show you that your brain cannot tell the difference between physical and emotional pain—to the brain, all pain is seen as being the same. Secondly, it should show you how powerful your thoughts are in bringing about physiological symptoms. One ugly thought has the power to change your mood, make you defensive, cause you to withdraw socially, and ultimately adopt fear-based beliefs about yourself, your life, and even people in your life.

If you are someone who suffers from undiagnosed anxiety, it may be hard for you to understand what's happening in your body or why you cannot seem to stop the negative mental self-talk. To put it plainly, your anxiety may cause you to feel like you're going insane or that nobody else will ever understand your experience. The truth is, you aren't going insane, and your experience is shared by millions of people around the world, the young and old, rich and poor, and even democrat or republican. Anxiety does not discriminate.

In this book, I show you how normal your anxiety is and that it's possible to live a life free from it. It took me many years to learn that battling with anxiety doesn't need to be a life sentence. You were never born anxious; your anxiety came as a result of internal and external experiences that have come and gone. What's left of the past is your anxiety, and I'm determined to give you strategies on how to eradicate it from your life, too. It takes courage to seek help and desire a healthier life for yourself, and if you're still reading this book, I know you are brave enough to confront your anxiety head-on.

A peaceful life isn't an illusion or childish fantasy. Take it from me—happiness and unrestrained freedom are awaiting you on the other side of your anxiety. If you are ready to take action and seek a new way of living your life anxiety-free, you will find this book truly valuable. In this book, I will take you through seven steps on how to control your anxiety and thrive in various aspects of your life, including your career, health, and relationships. However, to truly benefit from this book, I will need you to open your mind. Be willing to read the information that may or may not challenge your existing views. Be willing to try out the various exercises or tips I will share, even if you do them just once! Be willing to open your heart, and reflect on your own life experiences, as I share various stories of people I have encountered, who have suffered from anxiety and endured it. Be willing to accept that you don't have a solution for your anxiety yet, or admit that what you have tried in the past hasn't worked.

Your open-mindedness and honesty will help you make the most of the knowledge I intend on sharing with you.

Before we commence our journey together, please note all identifying facts of people mentioned in the stories have been changed to protect their confidentiality, and some stories may be shared experiences of different people. You should also note that this book does not replace therapy. If you are in the later stages of depression, I lovingly advise that you seek professional counseling before reading this book. Below are free U.S. anxiety

Why I Created the 7 Explosive Steps

helplines you can contact at any time of day or night:

- National Alliance on Mental Illness (NAMI) Helpline: 1-800-950-NAMI (6264)
- National Suicide Prevention Lifeline: 1-800-273-TALK (8255)
- Substance Abuse and Mental Health Services Administration (SAMHSA) Helpline: 1-800-662-HELP (4357)
- Teen Line: 1-310-855-HOPE (4673) or 1-800-TLC-TEEN (852-8336)

If you live in Canada, please contact the helplines below (Public Health Agency of Canada, 2020):

- Canada Suicide Prevention Service: 1-833-456-4566 (24/7) or text 45645 (4 pm to 12 am ET)
- Hope for Wellness Helpline: 1-855-242-3310 (toll-free) or connect online to the Hope for Wellness chat.

If you live outside of the U.S. or Canada, please reach out to your local crisis helpline association.

KNOWING YOUR ENEMY IN THE BATTLEFIELD

"My anxiety doesn't come from thinking about the future but from wanting to control it."

— Hugh Prather

I had a friend at school named Pam. Well, I like to remember her as my friend, but I don't think I knew much about her besides the fact that she thought she was fat. Pam and I sat next to each other in most classes, and she would write self-deprecating statements on post-it notes and send them to me to have a look at. I never really knew what to say, except to tell her those beliefs weren't true. She would laugh it off and continue with her classwork, but I could tell those statements came from a much deeper place.

Her behavior outside of class gave it away. Pam would stay as far away from the cafeteria and avoid people who were eating lunch. She would constantly try diets that challenged her to eat as few calories as she could. At some point, all Pam was eating was apples for weeks on end. I watched as Pam's body gradually shriveled until she became unrecognizable. Her belief that she was fat had caused Pam to fear gaining weight and ultimately led to an eating disorder. Teachers advised her parents to take her to a rehabilitation center for a few months so she could address her disorder, and they did.

This incident highlights the extremes of anxiety. Before then, I thought anxiety was having frequent panic attacks and troublesome thoughts about the future, however, I learned anxiety could also affect how you see yourself and cause you to adopt negative and self-destructive behavioral patterns. I realized I had only seen one side of this beast and never really knew how destructive it could get.

— Dillion

IT'S MORE THAN JUST WORRYING

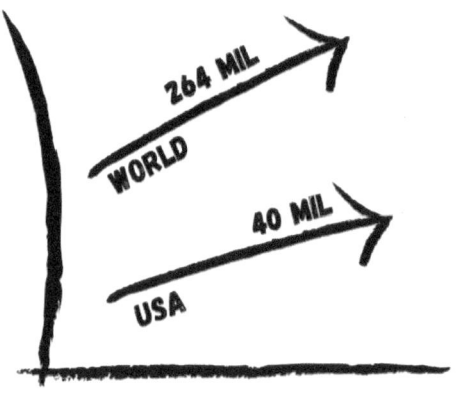

If you do a quick Google search and look at the synonyms that pop up for "anxious," you will find words like: concerned, uneasy, worried, and troubled. As much as anxious people can feel all of these emotions, these words don't adequately describe the experience of anxiety. Anxiety is more than being worried about a test or having the jitters before going on a date. Anxiety is a strong, and often crippling emotion that negatively affects your mental and emotional health, causing you to miss out on so many experiences in life.

Someone who is nervous and someone having an anxious episode may be going through two completely different experiences. While both of their hearts may beat really fast, the nervous person can still imagine themselves overcoming the obstacle, while the person having an anxious episode sees a dead end. I would also like to say there are so many levels of anxiety and therefore, not everyone's anxiety will look or feel the same. Before we go into the various types and manifestations of anxiety, let's define what it is.

In simple terms, anxiety is the body's response to fear. Since fear affects people in different ways, there is a vast range of how intensely anxiety may affect a person, or to what extent it interferes with their quality of life. According to the World Health Organization, it's estimated that over 264 million adults worldwide suffer from anxiety, and over 40 million of those adults live in the United States (Dershowitz & Hudson, 2021). The pandemic of 2020 has only exacerbated our anxieties as individuals and a collective society. Anxiety in itself isn't a mental health illness, however, it can sometimes develop into a mental health disorder and bring about various anxiety-induced disorders, such as:

Generalized Anxiety Disorder (GAD)

Generalized Anxiety Disorder is the most common anxiety-induced disorder. Usually, a person is diagnosed with GAD after suffering from anxiety, with very little to provoke it, for a period of six months. This prolonged state of anxiety affects many areas of the person's life, including their work performance, the quality of their relationships, and how they socialize with others.

Panic Disorder

Panic disorders describe unexpected and repeated panic attacks that a person may have, which causes them to withdraw or avoid certain situations, or frequently worry about when the next panic attack will occur.

Phobia-Related Disorders

Phobia-related disorders are characterized by the fear of an object or situation. Even though some of these objects or situations are fearful (like creepy crawlies or the fear of heights), a person with a phobia has a disproportionate amount of fear in relation to the actual danger or threat presented.

Obsessive-Compulsive Disorder (OCD)

People with obsessive-compulsive disorder experience recurring, unwanted thoughts or ideas that urge them to do something repetitively. Examples of common OCD behaviors include checking objects repeatedly to make sure one is safe, repeating a name or phrase because one is afraid something bad will happen if they don't or cleaning the house compulsively from fear of germs or contamination.

Post-Traumatic Stress Disorder (PTSD)

Post-traumatic stress disorder occurs when someone has difficulty recovering after a traumatic experience or period in their life. Symptoms of PTSD may last several months or continue for several years. Some of the common symptoms of PTSD include having recurring flashbacks about the past traumatic event, avoiding the people, places, and things that remind one of a past traumatic event, or feeling hopeless about the future.

STRESS VS. ANXIETY VS. DEPRESSION

Stress is not a new phenomenon that came with the 2020 pandemic. The stress response is something all human beings are born with, which plays an important role in our survival as a species and as individuals. Our primitive ancestors had different "life problems" than the ones we have now. They would stress about animal invasions or not being able to source any food. The stressors of modern humans are quite sophisticated. We stress over affording healthcare, how economic inflation will bring up the cost of food, whether our loan application will be approved, or even how we'll be able to protect ourselves from future pandemics.

Wherever stress abides, anxiety follows. Anxiety is more debilitating than stress. The mind takes what could've been a general sense of concern and whirls it into a storm of restlessness and fear. What's more is prolonged anxiety may lead to its more serious cousin, depression. According to the Anxiety and Depression Association of America, nearly half of people who are diagnosed with depression also suffer from an anxiety disorder (Raven, 2020). Many times, it can even be difficult for someone to tell the difference about whether they are depressed or suffering from anxiety.

I want to briefly speak about the three psychological states and offer a few tips on how you can address each one by adopting healthy behaviors.

Stress

In simple terms, stress is a physical response you get when the brain perceives danger. Your brain receives a threatening signal from the environment, and a flood of chemicals overwhelms the rational side of the brain known as the prefrontal cortex. At this point, you can no longer think logically about your next move. While this reaction is taking place, neurotransmitters like dopamine and norepinephrine rush into your amygdala, the part of your brain that's responsible for the fight-or-flight response. In essence, when you're experiencing stress, you lose all sense of reasoning and enter survival mode, ready to either confront the perceived threat or withdraw and hide.

Stress isn't necessarily unhealthy since it serves a biological purpose, however, what happens when the danger your brain perceives is a false alarm? For instance, what happens when your brain receives a threatening signal when attending a social event, going into a job interview, speaking to someone you have a crush on, or sharing your opinion in a boardroom meeting? Are these situations life-threatening? No, they aren't, but since your brain perceives anything fearful to be dangerous, these stressors can put you in a state of fight-or-flight mode. Prolonged stress leads to serious physiological symptoms, like migraines that come unexpectedly, insomnia, the loss of appetite, compulsive behaviors like grinding your teeth, and so on.

There are many ways to reduce stress and bring a sense of ease into your mind and body. Here are three basic actions you should consider in order to combat stress:

1. **Get active:** Exercise reduces stress hormones, like adrenaline and cortisol, in your body and loads you up on feel-good endorphins, which naturally elevate your mood.

2. **Get organized:** When your mind is overactive, you cannot think straight. Getting into a habit of writing your thoughts down on paper or scheduling your daily tasks can help you feel a sense of control amidst a chaotic time.

3. **Focus on the good:** In a stressful state, negative thoughts come naturally. One "What if" can lead to six more, and before you know it, you are caught in a loop of overthinking. Turn things around by focusing on the good things each moment offers. Look around you and count at least 10 good things you can see.

Anxiety

Anxiety shares the same biological and physical elements as stress, however, there's a slight difference between the two. Stress is usually caused by a lived experience, and anxiety is caused by an unknown factor. In other words, the situation looks fearful, but when analyzed, turns out to be harmless.

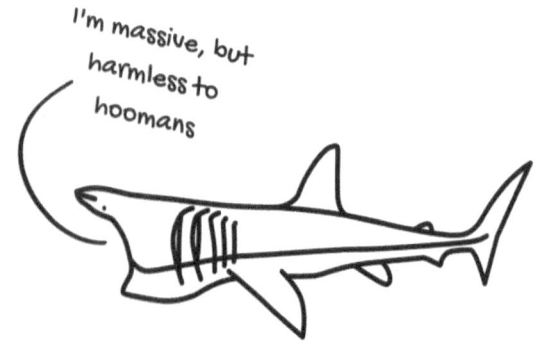

Have you heard about basking sharks? They are the second-largest species of extant shark, weighing 35,500 pounds, and they are significantly larger than the Great White shark (Buckley, 2020). These 40-foot-long sea creatures have jaws that can stretch three feet wide and look more deadly than any other fish. However, looks can be deceiving. Basking sharks may look monstrous, but they have a docile nature and no sharp teeth. These plankton-eating sharks have no desire to eat human beings, let alone any other large animal.

In many ways, our anxieties are presented in a deadly and threatening way, though after close examination, we find there was nothing to fear all along. Anxiety can also manifest as an overwhelming feeling that our inner strength and capabilities are no match for our environmental stressors. For instance, moving to a new job can trigger anxiety because one might feel unprepared for the new work environment and unknown challenges that may be presented.

Even though anxiety-induced fears are imaginary, anxiety triggers are real and based on everyday circumstances. Common anxiety triggers include losing a job, falling sick, separating from or losing a loved one, moving to a new city, facing financial difficulties, or receiving flashbacks from past traumatic experiences, just to name a few. Here are three best practices for dealing with anxiety triggers:

1. **Focus on the present moment:** Many anxiety attacks are caused by concern, or fear, of future events or scenarios. Bring your mind back into the present moment and ground yourself on what is here right now. Calm your mind by looking around you and finding five things you can see with your eyes, four things you can hear, three things you can touch, two things you can smell, and one thing you can taste.
2. **Practice self-compassion:** When you feel anxious, find ways to reassure your mind and body that you are safe. For instance, you can repeat to yourself, "I am safe in my body," until you feel your heart rate slowing down. You can also practice sitting with your emotions and feeling them, instead of judging or separating yourself from them. Acknowledge your emotional experiences, embrace them, and realize that they're only temporary.

3. **Realize what's in your control:** Not everything you're anxious about is in your control. There are some matters you cannot resolve in your personal capacity. Examples of these would be world hunger, a pandemic, or crime. By focusing instead on things you can control, you will be encouraged to think of reasonable solutions and take action.

Depression

When anxiety persists for a long time, it can become interwoven with depression, a mental health disorder that can manifest differently from one person to another but shares a common experience—the inability to enjoy all that life offers. Unlike stress or anxiety, very little is known about the mechanisms of depression except for the noticeable symptoms it brings about.

Knowing Your Enemy in the Battlefield

For instance, those who suffer from depression often lose the ability to function in one or more areas of their lives, which may include their work lives or in their relationships. This disorder can be deadly when it leads to suicidal thoughts or planning. What's even more disheartening, is that someone who already feels like a burden to others is less likely to reach out for help or to tell a close friend they are having these suicidal thoughts.

Even though depression is usually associated with grief, hopelessness, and anxiety, it's not always displayed in that way. Smiling depression refers to someone living with depression but who appears to be happy on the outside. They can perform at work and show up to social events without anyone noticing the bitter pain hidden within. People who demonstrate smiling depression often view their depressive feelings as a weakness and exposing them would humiliate or cause others to judge them.

For many people suffering from depression, seeking professional help is the first step toward recovery. Treatment for depression varies and may include a combination of therapy and prescription medication. Engaging in exercise can also help reduce the symptoms of depression, however, exercise will not cure depression.

Another suitable intervention would be making an effort to connect with other people, even when it feels better to self-isolate. An excellent exercise here would be for someone to write down the names of people they feel closest to, and next to each name, mention how speaking to or seeing that person makes them feel. Whenever the person sinks into a low mood, they can pull out their list and call the people who can lift their mood.

Even though stress, anxiety, and depression are different, they all speak to the same theme of feeling unsafe in one's environment or one's body. Addressing all three psychological states will require someone to first challenge the reason for feeling threatened, fearful, or out of control in their environment or body. This process takes a lot of time; however, the more awareness someone has about their mental state, the easier it becomes to find solutions and take action.

ANXIETY MEDICATION: TAKE IT OR LEAVE IT?

There are a variety of medications available to treat anxiety disorders. Most times, medication works well when combined with other interventions that address underlying psychological triggers, like therapy. Not everyone in the medical community agrees about the use of medications as a treatment for anxiety. Those against the use of anxiety drugs believe these pills aren't worth the side effects that come with them. Some of these side effects include jumpiness, decreased libido, and abnormal sleeping patterns. Instead, they believe modifications in behavior can significantly reduce symptoms of anxiety and, in some cases, free a person from anxiety for good. If you ask me, medication may help in the short term, but certainly cannot help you long-term unless you take steps to fix your life. Nonetheless, learning about the various medications available to you can increase your treatment options. I want to clarify that I am not a doctor, nor am I suggesting you take any of the following medications. If you feel you need additional help to cope with your anxiety or depression, please consult your health care physician.

Benzodiazepines

Benzodiazepines are common medication to treat anxiety and among the most prescribed by doctors around the world. When used appropriately, benzodiazepines can relieve a person from symptoms of anxiety, however, when abused, can become highly addictive. The most popular and commonly prescribed forms of benzodiazepines include Xanax, Valium, Restoril, Librium, and Ativan, to name a few.

Benzodiazepines work like other sedative drugs—by shutting down neurotransmitters and reducing tension and anxiety. Unlike most sedatives, these drugs only shut down cells responsible for worrying or thinking, and don't shut down the whole body. In extreme cases, these drugs can interfere with normal brain function, causing memory loss. Even after taking benzodiazepines for a few weeks, one can experience harmful withdrawal symptoms like seizures, panic attacks, insomnia, and ironically, increased anxiety.

Antidepressants

Antidepressants refer to a number of medications used to treat symptoms of depression. However, since these medications increase chemicals like serotonin and dopamine, they can also be used to treat symptoms of anxiety. The most common types of antidepressants are Selective Serotonin Reuptake Inhibitors (SSRIs). These include medications like Prozac, Zoloft, Lexapro, Paxil, and Celexa. When compared to benzodiazepines, SSRIs are less addictive because it typically takes four to six weeks before the effects start kicking in.

Even though antidepressants aren't addictive, users must be careful when taking them. For instance, abruptly quitting treatment or missing a few doses can cause withdrawal symptoms, like anxiety, dizziness, and fatigue. Additionally, in the four to six-week window where the body becomes used to the drugs, various symptoms, like suicidal thoughts, insomnia, or sexual dysfunction may occur.

Once again, if you are interested in taking any of the medications mentioned above, it's advised you speak to a medical professional first, so you can learn about the best treatment and dosage for you. Moreover, your treatment should be accompanied by various lifestyle and behavioral changes to address the underlying psychological causes of your anxiety. If you believe that you or a loved one may be self-medicating to treat symptoms of anxiety or depression, reach out to a medical professional and ask them about possible treatment options.

Pam returned to school after six months of treatment at a rehabilitation center. When she walked into the classroom, I recognized her by the big smile on her face. The old Pam was gradually coming back, and she looked a lot healthier. We cracked a few jokes to each other like we always used to, and I waited to see what note she would write to me on her post-its this time. A few minutes into the lesson, I saw a bright yellow post-it note from the corner of my eye. On it, Pam had written, "I accept myself," and I knew whatever treatment she had received from the center—and the therapy that came along with it—had helped her change the old perspective she had about her body.

PART 2

THE STEPS

EXPLOSIVE STEP #1

DECODING AND NAMING YOUR STORM

"Even in the midst of the storm, the sun is still shining."

— Dayna Lovely

After graduating from college, I was under the impression that recruiters would be blowing up my phone, competing among each other to have me at their particular firms. Oh boy, was I mistaken. I fell under the statistics of professional graduates sitting at home with degrees, due to the scarcity of jobs.

Explosive Step #1

Being unemployed was stressful enough, although feeling the external pressure to find a job led to constant anxiety attacks. I felt like a disappointment to my family because I couldn't show them that I could stand on my own two feet. I also felt embarrassed to be around my friends who had found jobs and were moving out of home, and some even to new cities. Alcohol gleamed at me, and recreational drugs became my best friend. No one noticed how miserable I was inside because I did a good job masking my pain with a smile.

When I would sit alone, my thoughts would trouble me. The critical inner voice in my mind would remind me of how much of a failure I was. At the time, I didn't have the strength to confront these thoughts. They seemed too powerful and too real for me to challenge. I would passively agree with every negative thing I believed, and because of this, my anxiety continued longer than it should have. I didn't realize these thoughts were merely negative suggestions, and I had the choice of either accepting them to be true or revealing how fake they were. The truth is, I was in a rut, but my temporary rock bottom didn't have to define who I was and what I was capable of achieving in my life.

Now I know better than to accept negative suggestions. I know that I have control over my mind and my mind doesn't have control over me. Over the years, I learned how to decode and name my anxiety as it manifests in different ways.

— Elizabeth

Explosive Step #1

IT'S OKAY TO FREAK OUT!

Decoding and naming your storm is step one out of the 7 Explosive Steps to control and cope with anxiety, and I am going to outline a detailed process for how you or a loved one can do it too. Life doesn't always go according to plan, and when you're suddenly having to put out fires you never started, it's okay to freak out! We've been taught to hide our true feelings and present a calm, cool, and collected external appearance, but have you ever wondered what happens to all of those strong feelings within you? Unfortunately, they don't evaporate and become non-existent; they wait for another strong emotional trigger to bubble up again.

What's the point of hiding what you feel anyway when many people can probably relate to the feelings you are experiencing? For example, the year 2020 will be on record as the year the entire world experienced a traumatic event. The pandemic affected every living human being on this planet, either directly or indirectly. Collectively, we felt hopeless as the virus spread like wildfire, with no known cure to treat it. When many people started losing their jobs, we were anxious about our own job security and how differently employment would look post the pandemic. Yet even in the midst of a global pandemic, there were many people who were afraid they would be judged for expressing their fears.

Explosive Step #1

I don't necessarily blame them for being afraid to truly express how they feel because our families and social circles are full of know-it-all personalities. I'm sure you can name a few in your own life. Someone who's a know-it-all believes they understand your life experience better than you do. They refuse to accept the fact that you may be going through a situation they are ignorant about. For know-it-alls, there is only one truth to live by in life and that's their truth.

Someone who experiences anxiety may struggle to express their feelings in front of know-it-alls because instead of listening and acknowledging what's being said, know-it-alls will provide their own reasonings and beliefs. For example, you might be anxious about being fired from your job because of the changing nature of the workforce, and a know-it-all would say, "Stop being dramatic." Another example is if you express feeling incompetent about your own abilities and a know-it-all—instead of listening and finding ways to understand your experience—tells you: "It's all in your head."

Like millions of people around the world, I used to think it wasn't socially acceptable to have a freakout. I thought it would be the "manly" approach to stomach my anxiety and pretend I could handle all of the pressure on my shoulders with ease. Everyone I admired seemed to be handling their business well and keeping smiles fixed on their faces, so I thought the least I could do is pretend to be happy like them. I didn't realize at the time that I was adding more pressure on myself by pretending to be "normal" when I didn't feel okay inside. Perhaps if I would have expressed the anxiety I was feeling (to people other than know-it-alls) I would've found many people who shared the same fears as I had.

Freakouts aren't as strange as we like to make them seem. Yes, sometimes they don't make sense, but does everything we do make sense 100% of the time? Sometimes, all you want to do is scream in a pillow or out loud to let off some steam, and that's okay. Get used to expressing yourself in different ways because that will come in handy in your recovery from anxiety.

IDENTIFYING ANXIETY TRIGGERS

Have you ever felt out of control over your body but didn't know why? When anxiety pays you a visit, it arrives suddenly and without any prior notice. Sometimes you will feel a wave of anxiety come over you during a conversation or after you have enjoyed a cup of coffee. Identifying anxiety becomes nearly impossible when we don't know what's triggering the anxiety. For all you know, you might be engaging in activities that trigger anxiety.

Here are five common triggers of anxiety for your consideration:

1. Caffeine

Caffeine is a stimulant and can aggravate the symptoms of anxiety (Iliades, 2018). The jitters some may get after drinking coffee are similar to the jitters one gets during or after a traumatic event. That's because caffeine activates the brain's fight-or-flight response, and this worsens or prolongs the symptoms of anxiety.

2. Heart Problems

If you have ever had a panic attack, you'll know what it feels like to experience shortness of breath, clammy hands, and how rapidly your heart beats out of your chest. Although in some cases, health issues with your heart may trigger anxiety. Research has shown people with generalized anxiety disorder (GAD) are at a higher risk of cardiovascular disease or getting a heart attack (Iliades, 2018).

3. Alcohol and Drugs

According to the Anxiety and Depression Association of America, about 20% of Americans who battle with anxiety or mood disorders, like depression, also have an alcohol or other substance abuse disorder (ADAA, 2021). Interchangeably, the abuse of alcohol and other drugs can lead to anxiety attacks or disorders. In other words, the combination of alcohol, drugs, and anxiety can be harmful to one's mental health regardless of which one manifests first.

4. Medications

Prescription and over-the-counter medication, such as cold and flu medicine or hormonal birth control, can lead to symptoms of anxiety. Moreover, when patients stop taking anxiety medication like benzodiazepines, anxiety can be triggered. Other health supplements known to trigger anxiety include weight loss pills or fat burners, which have anxiety-causing side effects. For instance, supplements with ingredients like green tea, guarana, or ephedra (for the suppression of appetite) carry a high dose of caffeine which can trigger heart palpitations and an anxiety attack.

5. Stress

Earlier in the book, we discussed the relationship between stress and anxiety. When you are grieving the loss of a loved one, facing challenges at work, or feeling financially insecure, the stress you experience can lead to anxiety attacks. Some people may even turn to alcohol or drugs to reduce the amount of pressure on their minds, and these mind-numbing substances may worsen the symptoms of anxiety.

Once you have identified your anxiety triggers, you are in a better position to address the underlying issues creating or aggravating the anxiety. For example, if you find after drinking a cup of coffee in the morning that you feel jittery, you can switch to a hot beverage with less caffeine content, like tea, or opt for a decaffeinated coffee option. It's also important for you to assess whether your triggers are truly anxiety-induced or perhaps due to chronic stress or depression. Refer once more to the comparisons of the three in Part 1 of this book, if you need to. You can also adopt a few healthy coping strategies to address your triggers, such as:

- **Writing in a journal.** If you enjoy writing down your feelings on paper, journaling may be a great way for you to calm your mind and identify the root of your anxiety. You can also write down effective coping strategies to refer to when you are experiencing a panic attack.
- **Identifying major stressors in your life.** Take a moment and think about the various circumstances occurring in your

life right now. As each circumstance pops up in your head, give it a rating out of 10 (with 10 being highly stressful) and determine which events are currently weighing heavy on your mind.

- **Reflecting and accepting past experiences.** When you avoid your past, you miss out on the opportunity to release old and toxic feelings. The past will always find ways of creeping into your present life experiences, causing you a lot of anxiety. By reflecting on your past and coming to a place of acceptance, you will no longer feel haunted by what happened to you.
- **Listening to your body.** Your body is a great source of information regarding your inner reality. Most of the time, mental health issues manifest physiologically in the form of migraines, loss of appetite, insomnia, fatigue, and so forth. If you are feeling a sense of heaviness or sadness, spend

time in prayer or meditation to realign your mind and body, and restore peace. You can also engage in other physical activities like yoga, swimming, or running, which will help your body return to its healthy state.

NAMING YOUR ANXIETY

Elizabeth remembers during her job-hunting days when she would experience an onslaught of negative thoughts every time she would apply to various job posts. These negative thoughts would suggest she was incapable of performing well in that job role, or that she was too introverted to work with other people in an organization. She would find herself having to sit with a knot in her stomach and try desperately to push back tears as she rejected herself before any recruiter could even look at her resume.

She could never understand why she felt like a failure even though she was actively trying to look for a job and claim her financial independence. Her negative thoughts never made any logical sense, but they were still highly influential in how she saw herself. She would call me names and mock every small effort she made to secure a job. Criticizing her personality was perhaps one of the defining characteristics of her anxiety. She judged herself ruthlessly, picking up on small faults that many of her friends or family members couldn't see.

She got to a point where she understood her anxiety trigger was due to being unemployed and staying at home. Reaching this revelation helped her look for coping strategies to address her anxiety. One of the coping strategies she found was to give the various manifestations of anxiety she experienced a name, just like hurricanes and cyclones are given names. Naming her anxiety helped her identify it quickly and separate it from who she was or from her current experience. For example, if she had an anxiety attack at a party, she would quickly identify it as Pastel (the name she chose), and let Pastel coexist for as long as she wanted without ruining her night or causing her to change how she responded to others.

Giving your anxiety a name humanizes it and makes it seem less like a monster. Since it has a name, it's also easier for you to think of it as being something separate from you. When anxiety suddenly hits, you can identify its personality without embodying the anxiety or its personality as your own. In some cases, people are able to completely remove anxiety from their lives; although, there are also cases where people experience anxiety in waves, coming and going whenever it pleases. In the latter case, naming your anxiety can help you build a healthy relationship with it, and remove all forms of resistance you have within that stops you from acknowledging and sitting with your anxiety until it disappears again.

Lastly, naming your anxiety helps you confront it and set boundaries with it. There are going to be times when an anxiety attack is inappropriate or can cause serious damage to your career or relationships. In those times, you can instruct your anxiety to calm down. A good example is when you are walking into a very important meeting where you need to present information to others. Before the meeting, you can take a moment to speak to your anxiety and tell it exactly what it can and

Explosive Step #1

cannot do in the meeting. You might say, "Sarah, I need you to stay calm in the meeting. I am going to present important information that requires me to focus and speak clearly. Please do not interrupt me during this meeting."

Giving your anxiety a name helps you gain back control over your mind. Regardless of where you might be, you can identify and speak directly to your anxiety, telling it who is boss. You are also likely to spend less time thinking about your anxiety or allowing it to fester into a bigger experience. Think of it as giving your anxiety an eye roll instead of fully focusing on it.

MINDFULLY SITTING WITH YOUR ANXIETY

If you desire to address your anxious feelings once and for all, it's important to first change your relationship with anxiety. Learn to think about anxiety differently and respond to it with a greater amount of compassion. You will notice how the anxiety shifts from having a domineering energy to one that is controlled. In other words, your behavior and perception about your anxiety predicts how the anxiety reacts in your body. When you surrender from fighting this emotion, and allow it to come and go whenever it pleases, the anxiety becomes less troublesome in your mind.

Remember, anxiety isn't always unhealthy—it has been biologically built into our bodies for a reason. There are going to be many instances in your life where feeling anxious can help you complete tasks skillfully, and with a greater level of concentration. Many years ago, I found that anxiety could be my friend if I learned how to handle it properly. As a friend, my anxiety could alert me whenever I needed to pay attention to something in my internal and external environment. For instance, not only could my anxiety alert me of new opportunities at work, but it could also alert me of my own fears and insecurities.

I forged a healthier relationship with my anxiety by learning how to "sit" with it until my anxiety attack had passed. I came up with a name for the anxious feeling I felt whenever I was around new people. His name was Dart. For many years, Dart was a menace in my life, causing me to socially withdraw from others and prefer self-isolation. However, I had reached a point where I wanted to befriend Dart so I could gently calm him down whenever I was part of social interaction. At first, I found it difficult to comfort Dart when he was having a full-blown tantrum, however, by learning to sit with him and feel whatever he was communicating to me, I was able to get through to him.

Just like no tantrum lasts forever, my anxiety attacks were able to fade away gradually. I realized all I needed to do in those vulnerable moments was to give my anxiety enough space to become what it wants to be, and it will eventually dissipate. I began a mindfulness meditation practice where I would stop everything I was doing and simply sit with my anxious thoughts, bringing them to my awareness, and giving them space to be. It wasn't easy having to feel all the strong emotions I had pushed down for so long, although after a few weeks of bringing up these emotions, I felt them lose their intensity. My experience with anxiety became less of a war and more about the transfer of information. My anxiety was sharing information I wasn't aware of, and I could acknowledge it and simply let it go.

Think of the sharing of information as a small toddler pulling at his mother's dress, trying to get her attention. The longer the mother ignores the toddler, the more frustrated and louder the toddler will petition. As soon as the mother turns her attention to the toddler and acknowledges what they want to share, the toddler immediately calms down and relays the message. Dart was much like a toddler whose mission was to get my attention when we were in public. By ignoring Dart, I was making his tantrum worse and causing a lot of unrest within me. However, as soon as I gave Dart the attention he needed and reassured him we were safe and there was no need to panic, I could enjoy my social interactions in peace.

When you notice yourself feeling anxious, take a moment to pause and think about the best ways to address your anxious feelings. Are you going to resist them or embrace them? Will you speak to your anxiety from a place of fear or compassion? Notice the ways your experience with anxiety changes as a result of choosing a different response.

I have four strategies that I like to consider when confronted with anxious feelings:

1. Think about Your Normal Reaction to Anxiety

Take a few minutes to think about how you usually respond when feeling anxious. Alternatively, if you feel anxious most of the time, notice your attitude toward your anxiety. Try to observe your relationship with anxiety without judging or labeling it. Simply notice the patterns of behavior and work toward accepting what it is.

2. Consider the Possibility of a Mindful Attitude Toward Dealing With Anxious Feelings

Imagine how it would look and feel like to respond to your anxiety with curiosity and openness. How do you think your anxious feelings would change if you adopted a mindful attitude? You can also think about the consequences related to your anxiety that you have endured with a fearful attitude. How has your fearful attitude toward anxiety impacted your health, career, or relationships? Consider the first step you would need to take to start opening up your heart and embracing your anxious feelings.

3. Sit With the Anxiety for at Least a Minute

Allow yourself to sit with your anxious feelings for at least a minute and observe as your anxiety builds. If you notice yourself breathing rapidly, slow down your breathing and maintain a state of calm. Using your breath, inhale love and compassion, and direct it to your anxious feelings. Visualize your anxious feelings being covered by warmth, love, and acceptance. Feel your anxious feelings as a part of your body, not an invader. Continue breathing slowly and appreciating whatever thoughts or feelings your anxiety raises. If you notice you are feeling afraid, send love to wrap around the fear. Show yourself the same compassion you would show someone else who was experiencing the same ordeal.

4. Continue With Non-Judgmental Observation of Your Anxious Feelings

Observing your feelings without any judgment increases your mindful curiosity about your emotions. Instead of escaping what you feel, you are eager to learn about where these feelings come from and the message they want to share with you. Mindful curiosity also helps you notice the bodily sensations that arise when you're feeling anxious (perhaps your heart beats faster or your muscles become tense). Notice whether your

Explosive Step #1

anxious feelings increase or decrease in intensity the more you bring your awareness to them.

When you learn how to sit with your anxious feelings, you will see they are not as threatening as they seem. You will start developing a greater degree of empathy for yourself, and you'll learn to accept your anxiety when it comes. If you listen to your anxiety, you will learn a lot of things about yourself and your inner reality. Apply mindful curiosity to find out what your anxiety is trying to show you. Remember, all emotions are temporary—this includes anxiety. Be patient with your anxious feelings when they come, and allow them to evolve and dissipate in their own time.

Here is a guided mindfulness meditation to help you sit with your negative thoughts and gently release them:

> Sit in a comfortable position, either on the floor or on a chair. Make sure your back is straight and your shoulders are relaxed. When you are ready, close your

eyes and focus on your breathing. Follow your natural breathing rhythm without trying to slow it down.

When you are ready, double inhale through the nose and follow with an extended exhale through the mouth (MacCormick, 2020). Repeat this pattern until all tension is removed from your body and you are feeling completely calm.

While focusing on your breathing, you may have thoughts arise in your mind. As each thought passes by, identify the emotions that are associated with them.

Naturally, your mind will gravitate toward negative thoughts. This is acceptable. As each negative thought arises, notice what you are feeling. Assess how intense your feelings are, and notice where your feelings travel in your body. Attach each thought with an emotion. Try to avoid labeling negative thoughts as "negative," but instead, use words such as sad, frustrated, lonely, or misunderstood.

After acknowledging each thought and identifying it with an emotion, let it go and bring your awareness to another thought. Do this until you have recalled every pressing thought in your mind. If a previous thought seeks to come up again, acknowledge it and feel it once more. You might identify it under the same emotion as you did previously, or alternatively, you might interpret it as another underlying emotion.

Bring your attention to your breath, and while taking slow and purposeful breaths, remind yourself that thoughts come and go. What you feel strongly about today may not hold as much influence in your life in a month's time.

With your eyes still closed, repeat any or all of the following phrases to yourself:

- I persevere through anything.
- I am a survivor.
- I am in control of my mind.
- I know I am not defined by my anxiety.
- I know thoughts are impermanent.
- I am in charge of my feelings and I enjoy this peaceful state.
- I am patient enough to endure anxiety attacks.
- I am comfortable and safe in my environment.

When you are ready, bring your awareness to your body and gently open your eyes.

EXPLOSIVE STEP #2

QUADRUPLING YOUR GRATITUDE

"I cried because I had no shoes until I met a man who had no feet."

— Helen Keller

I remember attending my first week at work after graduating and feeling rather anxious. I wanted to make a good impression in front of my colleagues so I could fit into the work culture as quickly as possible. During my first lunch break, I met a young guy who was working three jobs to sustain his family. He told me how his

Dad had met with an accident and could not go to work for at least a year. He was the only breadwinner in their household, responsible for his family of four.

Even as he was describing his life situation, I could tell he was so thankful for his family because they were the reason he was able to move forward in life. I guess he hadn't had a moment to process all of the emotions he was feeling, and subsequently, they all came pouring out during our conversation. Instead of us having a discussion about work, we ended up talking about the gift of having a family and being blessed with a phenomenal support system. He said to me, "I don't know what I would do without my family," and at that point, I could tell he was willing to overcome any obstacle fighting for the well-being of his loved ones. This also made me thankful about my life; that I was blessed with a single job that paid all of the bills at home, and that my family was safe at all times.

— Mark

Explosive Step #2

THE SCIENCE OF GRATITUDE

Whenever something good happens in your life, you are reminded to be grateful. However, practicing gratitude in times of difficulty can positively affect your mental and emotional well-being. Think of gratitude as being a feel-good pill you take when you want to see the rainbow amidst the storm. Your current life experience may be gloomy, but practicing gratitude can help you find the positive aspect or lesson in what you are going through. Sounds fantastic, right? The downside to all of this is that not everyone's brain is wired for gratitude.

For many people, gratitude doesn't come easy. They may be surrounded by opportunities or seated in a position of privilege, yet their brain's default is to dwell on the negative circumstances in their life. On the outside, it may look like these people have an attitude problem, although research suggests a lack of gratitude may have something to do with a person's brain, genes, or personality.

1. The Gratitude Gene

Genetics may explain why some people find it easier to express gratitude than others. According to Summer Allen (2018), Michael Steger and his colleagues of the American Psychological Association conducted a study with twins. The study found that identical twins, who essentially have the same DNA, showed similar levels of gratitude in contrast to that observed with fraternal twins, which suggests there may be a genetic component to gratitude.

Studies have also investigated the COMT gene, which is included in the process of recycling dopamine in the brain. Jinting Liu and his colleagues reported in the *Journal of Affective Disorders* that people with a variation of this gene experienced more gratitude, while people with another variation of the gene experienced less gratitude (Liu et al., 2017). The brains of the respondents with the "less grateful" variation of the gene showed a greater negativity bias. A negativity bias refers to having a stronger reaction to unpleasant thoughts and emotions over pleasant ones. The negativity bias also made these respondents more sensitive to negative life events and circumstances than positive ones.

2. The Gratitude Brain

Research has found differences in brain structure between people who were notably grateful and those who weren't. One study found people who were inclined toward practicing gratitude had more gray matter in their right inferior temporal cortex (Allen, 2018). This particular area of the brain has previously been linked to interpreting other people's intentions. This would essentially make them empathetic toward the experiences of others and find the silver lining in challenging life circumstances.

People who were more and less grateful also showed differences in their brain activity. A 2015 study carried out by Glenn Fox and his colleagues at UCLA asked participants to imagine they were Holocaust survivors who had received gifts of food and shelter from strangers. The participants who imagined they would be more grateful after receiving these gifts showed greater brain activity in areas associated with reward, moral cognition, and perspective-taking (Allen, 2018). Studies like these show us people who have altruistic brains have a tendency to show gratitude. However, it also proves that by training yourself to be considerate and compassionate toward others, you could train your brain to express gratitude.

3. The Gratitude Personality

While your genes and your brain can in some way influence your tendency to show gratitude, your personality can also serve as a promoter or barrier of gratitude. Have you heard about the "thieves of thankfulness?" These are personality traits that cause you to see nothing beyond yourself and your life experience. Examples of thieves of thankfulness are narcissism, cynicism, materialism, and envy. Let's break this down:

The Self-Serving Narcissist

Expressing gratitude in any way is beyond the capacity of the narcissist. A narcissist cannot identify with the good intentions of the gift-giver or selfless person because they struggle to show empathy. They are preoccupied with the "self" and cannot possibly see beyond their experience. Therefore, instead of feeling encouraged to give to others or express gratitude, they often feel like others owe them something or that they deserve the kindness and generosity shown to them.

The Suspicious Cynic

A cynical person is always suspicious of the motives of others. They feel as though expressions of kindness have an ulterior motive behind them. Even when a cynical person sees something beautiful, they find ways of diminishing its beauty by clouding it with negative truths and experiences. It can be difficult for cynical people to cheer themselves up when feeling anxious because they are inclined to believe the negative suggestions given to them by the anxiety. This prolongs the experience of anxiety and makes it very difficult to overcome it.

The Indulgent Materialist

There has been much research to prove that materialism reduces a person's level of contentment in their life. They may experience fewer positive emotions and can easily succumb to mental illnesses like anxiety, substance abuse, and depression. At the highest degree of materialism, people place more importance on possessions than on their own lives. For them, success is achieved by acquiring more things, and these possessions become the keys to happiness. This creates misery since, after acquiring one possession, the person is likely to aspire for another one, and another one, and so on. Thus, materialistic people are never satisfied with where they are in life or with what they have because their minds are always chasing more.

The Unsatisfied Envier

Envy is the act of idealizing a person or an object outside oneself, with the wish to own the object or live the person's lifestyle. Envious people cannot find peace within themselves because they always feel at a loss. This causes them to develop a hatred for others, especially those who they identify as better than them. When envy is strong, even what seems like an accomplishment or success in another person's life becomes a source of pain.

THE SECRET VIRTUE TO DEVELOPING A GRATEFUL HEART

Having a grateful heart is usually spoken of as being the starting point to good mental health and a prosperous life. A grateful heart isn't weighed down by the troubles of life because it understands that everything holds beauty in its own way. It doesn't look for joy beyond itself; instead of depending on other people to provide a sense of peace and happiness, it searches for these emotions within.

In today's fast-paced society, it can be difficult to not let the troubles of the day weigh you down. Nowadays, stress doesn't exist solely at work, it follows you to your home and in your social life. Even if you were to wake up feeling incredibly optimistic about the day ahead, the numerous challenges you face every day are enough to leave you feeling drained by the evening.

Explosive Step #2

Developing a grateful heart requires your input. Indeed, if you want to maintain a constant state of gratitude, you will need to possess the virtue of humility. Humility seeds, nurtures, and grows gratitude. Without a foundation of humility, gratitude will come and go as your feelings change. For instance, you might be grateful for receiving a lovely gift, but as soon the high fades away, the attitude of gratitude would also disappear. Humility isn't one of those virtues people chase after today. I guess it has to do with how culture has turned the focus on the individual, and daily life has become about ME. Caring for other people or things outside of yourself is seen as a sign of weakness or letting others control who you are.

Of course, this isn't true, and humility is anything but a weakness. For me, humility is the epitome of power. It opens your eyes to see you are only a speck of dust in the greater scheme of life. This doesn't dilute or minimize your life's challenges, but rather, it lets you see there is more to life than a temporary emotion or a temporary life circumstance. Humility helps you surrender to the current obstacles you are facing in life, not because you are powerless to them, but because you understand they are out of your control. What is the point of stressing about something you cannot change? Will thinking about it to the point of making yourself upset change the situation? Therefore, humility is all about putting down your mental weapons, accepting your current position in life for what it is, and learning how to mindfully sit with your anxious thoughts (refer to the mindfulness meditation script found under Explosive Step #1).

Humble people can at times be criticized for being too passive or insecure, however, those with a discerning eye will see how much confidence and self-awareness it takes to be a humble person. Jeff Boss, a former Navy SEAL, described a humble person best when he said, "To be humble is not to think less of oneself, but to think of oneself less."

Explosive Step #2

Five habits that will help you identify what humility looks like in a person are as follows:

1. They Have High Emotional Intelligence

Humble people are aware of their surroundings and how others perceive them but are not excessively obsessed with it. Their goal is not to please everyone, but to please only those they love and care about. They will not assert their beliefs or opinions on anyone else but will make sure their thoughts and feelings are voiced.

2. They Don't Take Criticism Personally

Humble people are able to laugh at themselves when they have made a mistake, and they don't get mad when criticized or rejected by other people. Once they move on from a situation, they are able to look back and learn lessons from it. It is this characteristic that helps them treat those who had previously rejected them with kindness.

3. They Are Others-Centered

A humble person will always make decisions that consider the interests of everyone involved. The last thing they would want is to make a decision that would negatively impact another person. To a humble person, life should always be a win-win situation, where everyone is growing and succeeding together.

4. They Are Curious

Humble people are eternal students of life. Even those with tertiary degrees still find ways of learning from each experience they encounter. The continuous dedication to learning keeps humble people grounded in who they are. At no point do they think they have all of the answers to their problems; instead, they are excited about gaining knowledge from people of all backgrounds and cultures.

5. They Aren't Afraid to Admit When They're Wrong

When a humble person catches themselves in the wrong, they aren't afraid to offer an apology. Saying "I'm sorry" isn't perceived as a sign of weakness for them because they recognize how powerful an apology can be in strengthening relationships. Humble people are also more likely than their prideful counterparts to empathize with people. Being able to put themselves in another person's shoes makes it easier to ask for forgiveness and seek reconciliation.

THE POWER OF POSITIVE REPETITION

For many years, I wondered why motivational speakers would constantly mention the power of positive thinking. In their videos, I would frequently hear them say, "Be positive," "Think good thoughts," or, "Look at the bright side of life." When I began practicing positive thinking, I could feel a noticeable difference in my mood. One of the most effective habits I have built is that I started a routine of waking up in the morning and repeating a few positive affirmations. Some of the positive affirmations I would repeat included:

- I am blessed to have a powerful support system; I live to make them proud of everything I do.
- I am fortunate to wake up and do the kind of work I do, and I don't take that for granted.
- My challenges are opportunities for growth, not things to complain about.
- I look at the past only to learn lessons, so I can build a better future.

It took me less than five minutes to repeat these affirmations in the morning, but the effects would last me the entire day. The changes in my mood occurred gradually. I felt less triggered by rude people I would come across while commuting to work or frustrated by my colleagues. I would describe it as having an invisible force field around me that protected me from negativity. Practicing positive affirmations showed me the power of positive repetition. I figured if my thoughts could shape how I felt, they could shape my future.

Let's consider practicing gratitude as an example. When you express how grateful you are for a person or an object in your life, it makes the person or object feel that much more valuable. Now, imagine expressing gratitude during a really difficult time in your life. How do you think it would make you feel about your situation? I would assume expressing gratitude would make the difficulty in life seem less overwhelming to bear, and it would also help you see the situation in a more positive way.

Positive repetition is speaking about what you hope to see more of in your life. Instead of telling everyone about how miserable your life is, positive repetition would encourage you to speak on the positive changes you hope to see. This would help you develop a positive mindset that would act as an invisible force field around your mind, safeguarding you against negativity. Without having to deal with negative thoughts, you could find coping with stress or anxiety a lot more bearable.

Besides repeating positive affirmations, there is another way of incorporating positive repetition in your life. Self-talk can help you remind yourself to think positively whenever you sink into a depressive thought. Simply put, self-talk is the ability to address the suggestions made in your mind (these include both positive and negative suggestions). Your mind will make thousands of suggestions every day, and you can co-sign and approve the suggestions you want to think and feel more of. For example, if you are overwhelmed with the piling workload at work, your mind may suggest two things: that you are in the wrong profession or that your increased productivity will soon pay off. Self-talk gives you the opportunity to speak what you want to think and feel more of. If you want to have a generally positive outlook on your job, you might prefer speaking positively about your increased workload.

This also presents another challenge: You need to learn to pause and take a moment to think before you speak. As I've mentioned before, words are extremely powerful in shaping your reality. By taking time to first think about how you want to respond to a situation, you can process a thought, weigh your options, and only speak what you desire to see. Thinking before you speak may be valuable when you are experiencing an anxiety attack or when you are trying to express yourself in a highly emotional situation. The natural tendency is to say whatever comes to your mind, however, we know better than to do this. The better option is to regulate your breathing (inhale for breaths and exhale slowly for one breath) and think about the best way to get your message across whilst speaking what you desire to see.

For example, you might feel like your friend has disrespected you by sharing information you expected them to keep in confidence. It's normal and expected for you to feel angry, betrayed, or deeply hurt. However, what you choose to say to your friend can and will determine the future of your friendship. By choosing your words wisely, you can clearly express how you feel and how your friend's actions have impacted your relationship with them, while also ensuring your friendship remains intact and able to survive this temporary storm.

Paying attention to your self-talk will improve the relationship you have with yourself and others. It will also help you encourage yourself whenever you slip into negative thinking or experience an unforeseen situation that seeks to destabilize you. Some people practice self-talk by speaking to themselves aloud, while others prefer to speak to themselves in their minds. Both approaches are powerful and can help you repeat positive messages to yourself throughout the day.

Here are 10 ways that you can develop positive self-talk with yourself:

1. Always See the Bigger Picture

Daily stressors can sometimes cause you to forget the bigger overarching goals in your life. If you don't have a big goal driving you in your career, health, or relationships, perhaps it's time to create one. Having overarching goals in your life will help you focus on the bigger picture when you are feeling discouraged. For instance, if you are frustrated with your slow-moving weight loss journey, you can remind yourself of your ultimate dream body or the kind of feeling you hope to have about your body. Speak about your goal in your conversations or spend time thinking about it when you are feeling discouraged.

2. Distance Yourself from Overly Negative People

Everyone complains or finds reasons to criticize others every once in a while, however, people who are overly negative do it constantly. If you are surrounded by Debbie Downers, it's time to walk away from them and spend more time with people who are also seeking personal development. The moods of negative people are contagious and if you stay around them long enough, you will develop the same defeated attitude they have. It's hard to completely cut negative people from your life, especially if they are coworkers or family members, although you can limit the amount of time you spend around them.

3. Choose to Look at the Brighter Side of Things

By choosing to think positively about things, you can significantly improve your attitude about life and have a greater appreciation for what you already have. Yes, life isn't perfect but that doesn't mean we shouldn't enjoy where we are and the road toward success. Take it from me, the more you practice positive thinking, the more confident you will be about who you are. Even amidst stressful times, you will be able to speak positively about your life circumstance and find the inner strength to overcome the present challenge.

4. Avoid Comparing Yourself to Others

Comparing yourself to other people can make you look at your life as being beneath somebody else's life. Is this a fair perspective to have? No, it isn't. Your life's path is very unique, and the only way your life makes sense is when you focus on the ways you have grown over the years and the milestones you hope to reach. By taking all of the energy you would put into focusing on another person's life and investing it in yourself, you will find so many wonderful things to be proud of and speak positively about.

5. Believe in Your Success

I learned a long time ago that I needed to be my own cheerleader in life. If I wasn't going to encourage myself, who would? You see, people take a long time to fully understand your path and the wonderful goals you are reaching for. If you wait on receiving validation from other people, you might feel discouraged to follow your heart and pursue your dreams. If you have a strong belief about something, affirm it to yourself and do everything in your power to incorporate your belief in how you live. You deserve to be successful, however, no one besides yourself will motivate you enough to pursue a successful life. Remind yourself often how intelligent and talented you are, and use the boost of confidence to fuel your goals.

6. Make Time for Daily Reflections

Spend 10 minutes of your morning or evening (depending on whether you are an early bird or a night owl) thinking about all that you have that many others do not. Think about the material possessions you have accumulated over the years, the school that you go to, the skills that you have acquired, the years of experience you have under your belt, how complex your mind is, or how kind you are—being thankful you never turned out to be the jerk who refused to help an old woman down the street.

7. Watch Your Language and Tone

When your Mom calls, stop yelling "What do you want from me?" and instead try responding with, "Yes Mom, how can I help you?" Communicating how you feel has a lot to do with the way you say something rather than what you say. Learning to watch your language and tone is all about conditioning your mind to respect others and choosing positive words that help you convey what you desire to see. Moreover, if you are someone who has developed a habit of filling sentences with swear words or speaking with a gloomy tone of voice, try being mindful every time you do it, and learn a new vocabulary if necessary!

8. Read or Listen to an Audiobook on Gratitude

I don't expect you to remember everything I have shared so far about gratitude. Feel free to refer to this section of the book whenever you need a pick-me-up or reminder of what gratitude looks and feels like. If you are an avid reader, you can also read books on how to cultivate gratitude and adopt a positive mindset. Knowledge about gratitude will open your mind, help you question your existing bad habits, and make the necessary changes.

9. Do Daily Appraisals

At the end of each day, ask yourself what you did that made you proud and what you can focus on improving. The truth is, no one is perfect, and there will be times where you yell at a loved one or carry a negative mood throughout the day. However, it's better to focus on the small positive steps you are taking to improve your mindset than to think about all of the mistakes you have made during the day. If you are unhappy with how you handled a situation, think of it as an area to improve on rather than something to criticize yourself about. Also, if you notice you have made significant improvements in certain areas, find ways of celebrating your victories, even if it's taking yourself out for ice cream.

10. Finally, Express Gratitude!

If you want to develop positive self-talk, it's imperative you develop and express gratitude. Gratitude is by far the best way of adopting a positive mindset and keeping your mental health in check. Learn to find different things every day to be grateful for. If you cannot think of anything to be grateful for, consider how differently your life would be if certain things or people were taken away. For example, if you rely significantly on your car, how would you feel if it was taken away? If you have found your soulmate and feel a great sense of appreciation for them, how would you feel if they were taken away? Thinking about your life from this perspective can help you identify people, places, and things that carry a lot of value in your life. Remember to regularly tell those you love how much you appreciate them.

EXPLOSIVE STEP #3

SMASHING OUTLIER EVENTS

"Never make a permanent decision about a temporary situation."

— T.D. Jakes

When I landed my dream job, I could hardly believe it. I was working in an industry I had always dreamed of developing my career in, and it was exactly as I had imagined it to be. Going to work didn't feel like an energy-sapping activity, however, my social anxiety got the best of me when I had to interact with my colleagues. I thought to myself, "Isn't there a way to socially isolate myself in this large and open office?" If I was given the opportunity back then, I would've found a snug corner, set up my workspace there, and spent my working days alone.

I felt different from my peers. Yes, we all had the same qualifications and had knowledge of the same skills, but a negative suggestion in my mind told me, "You don't deserve to be here." For a moment, I entertained this negative suggestion. Perhaps it was true—I didn't belong to be there. It was just dumb luck and something I should be eternally grateful for. But on the other side, I had worked hard to land that position and I couldn't discredit the previous sacrifices I had made to get there.

Was I a fraud? Was I stealing somebody else's position? The answer was NO. I deserved to be there and pursue the kind of career I dreamed of. Even though I was the new fish in the sea, I knew the ocean was big enough for me

Explosive Step #3

to swim in. Maybe my career wasn't as established as the rest of the folk there, but I believed I had the same opportunities to succeed at work as they did. No longer was I going to look at outlier events in my past and consider myself unworthy. The truth is, I am more than capable of being the best at what I do and I was finally ready to prove it!

— Joshua

WHEN AN OUTLIER ISN'T COOL

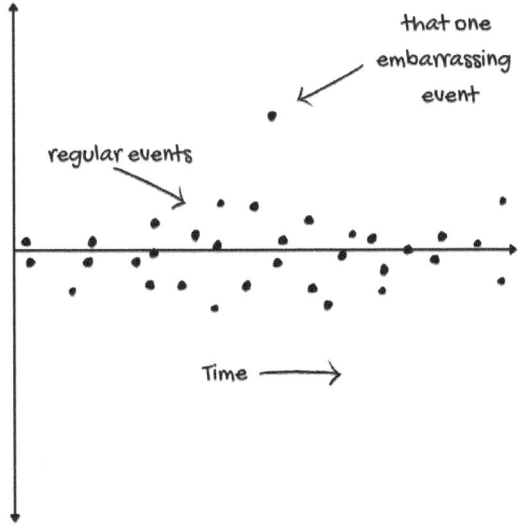

In the world of statistics, you want to look for a general pattern and any outliers in any given data set. An outlier is a data that doesn't fit into the overall pattern of the rest of the data. It's sometimes referred to as an extreme value. For instance, outliers can either be extremely lower or higher than the rest of the data, which can skew your analysis. Outliers stick out like a sore thumb because they go against the flow and don't appear to fit in with the rest of the pattern.

Consider a custom iPhone that costs $2,000 you find in a group of iPhones that range from $500 to $1,000. The average price of an iPhone in this group can skew higher solely because of the extremely high value of the outlier. This would negatively impact your results because it wouldn't show you the true average cost of an iPhone, and it would cause you to make a misinformed purchasing decision. The best way to fix this would be to remove the outlier and average your data set again.

Take a few minutes to travel to your past and think of a situation that was so catastrophic, traumatic, or embarrassing that it left you in tatters. It might have been a car accident, a horrible breakup, or being fired from your job. When you have connected to the memory, I would like you to connect with how you felt in the moment, as it was happening.

Remember to sit with your emotions and feel whatever arises within you.

Did you feel scared, disappointed, or angry? Who was there with you when it happened? What role did these people play or fail to play? Lastly, I want you to think about the ways your life has been impacted by this single outlier event. Think about the places, people, or things you are afraid of because of that single experience. What beliefs did you adopt about yourself or others after going through that event? And how have those beliefs impacted how you live today?

The issue with outlier events is they don't follow the predictable pattern of life. Usually, outlier events occur suddenly and can cause havoc in your calm and stable life. One example is how a pandemic impacted the world at large. I mean, who could've seen a global pandemic coming at the beginning of 2020? No one had made plans to save up money, buy sanitizers in bulk, wear masks, or stock up on food because there had never been an event carrying such a significant impact as this one. One single event caused shock waves in communities, workplaces, and households. Not only were people contracting an airborne virus, but they were also getting laid off from work or experiencing stress in their relationships.

If you aren't careful, you can shift your perspective to accommodate an outlier event. This wouldn't be a wise decision since outlier events are random and don't follow a pattern. Even though the pandemic forced us to adapt to a new way of interacting with the world around us, it would be wrong of us to strictly replace our lifestyles to accommodate the possibility of another global pandemic hitting us in the future. In other words, outlier events cause a mental shift in our minds, but if we don't work toward bringing our minds back to the regular patterns we know and trust, we will be constantly triggered by the horror or fear that struck us unaware.

I know many people who are terrified of leaving their homes since the global pandemic struck. Not only that, they are paranoid about reuniting with their friends and family. This creates a lifestyle of self-isolation which is unhealthy for human beings. We are naturally social creatures!

I also know of many people who are terrified of the future. They cannot seem to find any rest in the present moment because their minds are constantly trying to predict the next traumatic incident. I doubt that there will ever be another event like the pandemic during our lifetimes, and even if we experience another global pandemic, it will look completely different from what we have witnessed in the space of two years. None of us can plan our lives around outlier events because they are too inconsistent with the natural flow of life. The only thing we can do is work on dealing with the shockwaves and emotional distress caused by the outlier event.

Explosive Step #3

OVERCOMING THE FEAR OF THE UNKNOWN

The development of the 2020 pandemic brought about worldwide uncertainty. Previously, only those who were struggling to get by financially, or those who were in unstable relationships, felt uncertainty. The pandemic became the great equalizer between rich and poor, educated and uneducated, and single and married folk. I've never seen so many people relate to one another to the degree that they did during the spread of the pandemic. The unfortunate part is that we were bonding over fear and not love. Societies across the world were fearful of the outcome of the pandemic and how it would change life as they know it.

People dealt with the uncertainty of the pandemic differently. Some chose to steal and commit crimes out of desperation, others took their anxieties to the streets in protests and mass demonstrations, and there were also those who internalized their uncertainty and developed severe stress, anxiety, and depression. In short, the pandemic uncovered one of man's greatest weaknesses—the fear of the unknown.

The psychological term for the fear of the unknown is agnostophobia. Hailing from the Greek word *agnostos*, meaning "unknown," agnostophobia refers to anything or anyone that's unknown or unfamiliar. This type of fear is irrational in many ways since it comes about when people have very little information about the situation or a group of people, on any level. When the fear of the unknown is triggered, people can feel intensely anxious about a scenario that hasn't occurred yet. Just the thought of this scenario happening can cause them to develop an intolerance for uncertainty.

There are also times when the fear of the unknown is caused by recalling an outlier event, and fearing that it can happen again. For instance, if you applied for job interviews a hundred times and got rejected for each one, you might fear the possibility of facing rejection on the 101st job application. This also occurs when people meet a potential soulmate after experiencing a devastating breakup. They are terrified of opening up to the new person in their life due to the fear of going through similar heartbreak.

There are two major causes for the fear of the unknown:

1. Lack of Predictability

When you don't have enough information about a situation or opportunity, it may seem fearful. Your mind immediately generates "What if" scenarios that make you fearful of the possibility of rejection, failure, or death. Not being able to predict the outcome of your actions or environmental factors can raise your anxiety. The best way to calm your anxiety is to educate yourself on that which you fear the most. If you have been out of the dating game for a while, read a dating book or listen to YouTube videos that can prepare you on how to navigate the dating scene. Likewise, if you fear contracting an illness, educate yourself on prevention tips and how to maintain good health.

2. Lack of Control

Despite the fact that there is very little within our control, nobody wants to feel out of control. Feeling out of control can cause anxiety since it threatens a person's ability to survive. For example, when you feel insecure about your finances, it can cause you to feel uncomfortable about your future and your ability to take care of yourself. Regulating your fear of the unknown requires you to focus on the things within your control and put less pressure on your mind to figure out the things you cannot control. You may not be able to control your job security, but you can control your productivity and attitude at work, which can make you a valuable asset to your company.

When there's too much uncertainty around us, we tend to perceive our environment as threatening. If we cannot physically escape from our environment, we will retreat internally by emotionally checking out. The fear of the unknown can also cause us to perceive the future as threatening and everything new as being dangerous or untrustworthy. Learning how to cope with high levels of uncertainty can help us cope with anxiety in a healthy way. It can help us learn to be comfortable with disorder in our environment, without it affecting our mental health. For instance, we may not be able to control the rise in inflation or the possibility of falling into another recession, but our acceptance of uncertainty helps us make the necessary adjustments and manage change appropriately.

To live happy and healthy lives, we have to admit to ourselves that there are so many things we are uncertain about and every once in a while, we will be confronted with an outlier event that makes us doubt the very foundation we have built our lives on. However, life was never meant to be certain in the first place. The only thing promised to us in this lifetime is change, and this change can take us on so many different journeys. Change (whether it's the change we want to see or the change we fear) is instrumental in our growth as people and can help us become better versions of ourselves. Therefore, we never have to feel pressured to know what to do or how to react in every circumstance because the outlier event can teach us everything we need to know about that particular phase in our lives.

It's possible to sit with uncertainty and still find peace in your life's journey. There are three strategies you can practice to be comfortable with uncertainty and embrace change:

1. Normalize Feeling Bad

People are so good at masking negative emotions and only expressing positive emotions they feel are socially acceptable. I've learned the more I hide negative emotions, the more they screw me over in the long run. Let's face it, negative emotions are just as valid as positive ones. There isn't a secret hierarchy of emotions; all of them serve a really significant purpose in your life. Ignoring the built-up resentment you have been carrying since childhood will only make establishing healthy relationships fearful. It's okay to express fear, anger, or confusion. By expressing these strong emotions, you can reduce your anxiety about the future. Normalizing feeling sad or frustrated can also help you build your resilience to uncertainty. Once you have worked through how you feel about an uncertain event, the event will never trigger you as strongly as it did initially.

2. Develop Healthy Habits and Routines

The best way to manage uncertainty is to focus on the things you can control. Your habits and daily routine are in your control, and so is the overall attitude and mindset you have about your life. Choosing to develop positive habits that promote a positive mindset can motivate you to endure uncertain times. Developing positive habits and routines can empower you to improve on the areas of your life you have control over. If health is one of your goals, you can adjust your diet and incorporate more exercise in your weekly routine; this would make you feel a lot more confident about your overall well-being.

3. Think Creatively About Your Future

Since you don't have control of the future, you can spend your time visualizing the best possible scenarios instead of the worst. Instead of thinking, "What if I fail", think about the possibility of achieving your goals and living the kind of lifestyle you hope for. Consider how you would feel if you actually succeeded in your plans. Connect with the pleasurable emotions of winning at something and being victorious. Train your mind to always consider the brighter side of things and to be open to new opportunities that may lead to successful outcomes.

Explosive Step #3

OVERTHINKING AND THE FEAR OF FAILURE

There's a difference between planning for the future and overthinking every single detail to get there. When you plan for the future, you may create goals and a strategy on how to reach these goals. In the back of your mind, you are aware that life is unpredictable, and you may have to adjust your goals along the journey. However, when you overthink every single detail about your future, you can trigger anxiety. Why? Well, first, there is no certainty that your future will look as you imagine it to, and second, you create an unrealistic expectation of how you want your life to turn out.

Overthinking, in general, has become a common mental activity for most people. This is because society has developed at such an accelerated rate, that people are having to aim higher and take on more responsibility as a way to keep up with the changing times. Now more than ever, people are having to juggle growth in their careers, while simultaneously raising families, and making time to prioritize their health. Sounds like a lot, right? In the practice of meditation, regulating your breath is a key component to relaxing your mind and body. When your breathing slows down, your muscles loosen up, and your thoughts are able to detangle and flow loosely in your mind. Practices like meditation have become more popular in recent years because many people have been seeking ways of slowing down their mental machines.

I don't blame people for falling into loops of these thoughts. Think about it this way: If you had many fires to put out, wouldn't you want to prioritize each fire at the same time to prevent yourself from burning? If we were facing only one challenge in our lives, perhaps we wouldn't feel the need to overthink it; however, we are facing many pressures in our lives that force us to try and come up with interventions so we can maintain our sense of stability.

There are going to be times where we can overthink our past failures. When presented with new growth opportunities, we may think about the last time we tried to succeed and failed, and this may deter us from trying again. No one enjoys rejection or feeling like a failure, but many times, overthinking can cause us to feel like failures before we have even tried or put effort into our plans. For example, someone who desires to lose weight may think back on a time they went on a diet to lose weight and gained the weight back within weeks. This memory may cause them to fear losing weight by dieting, and thus, they may decide to not pursue weight loss altogether. This example shows how overthinking bad experiences can cause us to delay or forfeit our goals and remain in the comfort zone.

The only place overthinking doesn't exist is in the comfort zone, but opportunities and growth cannot be found in the comfort zone either. In other words, we need to become comfortable with being uncomfortable to access new opportunities and experience growth. This means we also need to be comfortable with having doubts and not being fully convinced about our plans. Overthinking isn't necessarily a bad thing when we recognize that we are overthinking. For example, if someone is about to go into the dentist's room, their mind may think of a million things that may go wrong. However, if they are aware that their thoughts are a product of overthinking (because of their fear of the dentist) they will be able to sit down on the dental chair and calm their nerves as the dentist begins their work.

Thus, being able to recognize when we are overthinking can cause us to have enough courage to continue with our plans, despite our fears or reluctance. It can also make us comfortable with the possibility of experiencing outlier events or having our plans change. Earlier we spoke about naming and speaking to your anxiety, but did you

Explosive Step #3

know you can also speak to your mind? If you are overwhelmed with an influx of thoughts, you can instruct your mind to calm down and process each thought, one at a time. It's a lot easier to acknowledge a single thought and give it the attention it deserves, than trying to process multiple thoughts and dividing your attention among them. Practices like meditation, prayer, reflection, and journaling can also help you slow down your mind and process each thought, one at a time.

Now for the good news: Overthinking isn't a mental condition, it's merely a bad habit! I remember a time when I told myself to stop thinking about eating ice cream and to my surprise, all I could think about was going to the store and buying the biggest tub of ice cream I could find. So clearly, trying to resist or avoid certain thoughts isn't the best strategy to follow. You can break the cycle of overthinking, however, and train your mind to look at life differently, with a more empowered and positive perspective. Healing your mind from overthinking involves replacing the anxious thoughts with inspiring ones. Instead of telling your mind that certain thoughts are forbidden, you can consciously focus on the quality of thinking you desire to see more of in your life.

If I wanted to stop thinking about eating ice cream, I should've rather focused on thinking about something I really wanted to start doing, like going on walks around my neighborhood. By replacing one thought for another, I wasn't necessarily telling my mind that thinking about ice cream is bad, but I was promoting a thought I felt was better or more valuable. You can tame your overthinking by regulating what you think upon. Overthinking the status of your relationship with your significant other, for example, will cause you a lot of anxiety (not to mention confusion). Instead, you can replace these thoughts with positive thoughts about how your significant other makes you feel. Choosing to focus on the latter will make you feel more confident in your relationships and bring peace to your mind, whereas

Explosive Step #3

focusing on the negative aspects of your relationship might just create unnecessary problems.

F.A.I.L.

I once knew a woman named Diana. She was the epitome of a hard-working and ambitious career woman. She was fortunate enough to attend an Ivy League university and graduate top of her class. During her final year of studies, she was headhunted by one of the globe's leading consultant firms. Within five years of working at the firm, Diana had been promoted three times and held an executive position. While all of this amazing career growth was happening, Diana was also getting to know a man who would later become her husband. As happy as she was succeeding in her career, she didn't see herself enjoying her career success without having a family by her side. Thankfully, her husband desired to have a family just as much as she did, and within three years of meeting each other, the pair were married.

Diana and her husband never got the opportunity to enjoy their honeymoon because both of them had to report to work as soon as the wedding ceremony was over. I remember listening to how invested Diana was in her career and wondering how on earth she was able to still make it home by six in the evening and cook a delicious homemade meal from scratch. The closer I got to Diana, the more I saw she was a perfectionist by nature. She saw herself as a superwoman who could pretty much do anything she set her mind on. I don't disagree with this, however, sometimes I think Diana forgot she only had 24 hours in a day. She was passionate about being a highly successful career woman and a devoted wife, but seeking to be perfect in these roles would soon bring devastating outcomes.

About a year into their marriage, Diana's husband wanted them to expand their family and plan on having children. Diana, being the perfect wife, agreed with her husband, and within months, they were expecting a baby. Diana had a way of making pregnancy look easy. Up until the eighth month of her pregnancy, she was the first to enter the office, and the last to leave. When their baby arrived, Diana and her husband adjusted well in the first few weeks of being parents. However, when the baby was three months old, Diana was diagnosed with postpartum depression.

As a new mother, she felt overwhelmed with the responsibility of taking care of her newborn. Raising a child turned out to be a completely different ball game than applying strategy in the world of business. Never before had she felt so out of control and helpless in providing what her baby needed. When I spoke to her later on, she told me that her goal when the baby arrived was to be a perfect mother. She felt like this goal was achievable since she was able to succeed in other aspects of her life. But the reality of being a parent was one far from perfect. Her baby would cry uncontrollably, and for the first time in her life, she didn't know what to do. Diana's ambitions of being a perfect mother soon tired her out and she decided to get counseling.

— *Sarah*

Perfection is the enemy of progress. Many times we aim for extravagant goals, or an extravagant lifestyle, and forget about the smaller victories we are making to move our lives forward. It's good to be ambitious and desire more for your life, but sometimes your ambition can cause you to be blind to the positive changes you have made in your life thus far. I often find those who seek perfection were usually brought up in households or communities where failure was not an option. Perhaps they had parents who expected exceptional academic results or exceptional social etiquette. Many parents believe they are doing their children a favor by setting high expectations for them to achieve, but in reality, their children grow up to become adults whose success and happiness are tied to external achievements.

Perfectionism can be damaging in many aspects of your life for two reasons. First, seeking perfection is a futile goal because perfectionism is subjective. You can never really reach perfection because what's deemed excellent for one person may be average for another. Second, seeking perfectionism can be damaging because it robs you of a grateful heart. I have seen many professionals sleep at the office, miss their children's recitals, and live on energy drinks just to achieve career goals and climb up the corporate ladder. Is it really worth it? That's a question you will need to answer for yourself, but I'm always wary of plans or goals that compromise my mental, emotional, and physical well-being.

One of the reasons people seek perfection is because they are afraid of failure. Failure can be described as a lack of success or not being able to complete a desired action. However, the less conventional definition of failure is "first attempt in learning," or F.A.I.L. I have found in my own life that how I choose to perceive failure can influence my attitude toward my current life circumstance. At all times, I have two options: I can either perceive failure as being the roadblock that stops me from attempting to pursue my goals, or I can see it as a necessary learning curve to help me refine my goals. Moreover, I can also perceive the delays caused by failure in two ways. Either I can see these delays as being a sign from heaven that I shouldn't be pursuing my goals, or I can see the delays as being a sign from heaven that I should take another look at my strategies and gather more information about how I can execute my goals efficiently.

Many people are unaware of their options when it comes to addressing and overcoming failure. This is why we see people quitting before they have accomplished their goals or procrastinating in the middle of pursuing their goals. No one really told us we could choose to perceive failure in a positive way. For as long as I've lived, failure has always had negative connotations associated with it. Thankfully, I have been empowered to make a choice to not let failure get in the way of me achieving the success I hope to achieve. Since you are now aware that you have a choice, you can also choose to see failure in a positive light and use it as a springboard to launch you into the next phase of your journey.

Let's practice seeing failure in a positive light, shall we? If you were to write a business proposal and your proposal was rejected at the bank, how would you handle this public display of failure? Here are your options:

A: Thank the banker for their time and go to another bank seeking the same type of business loan.

B: Throw your business proposal in the trash and forget about your entrepreneurial ambitions.

C: Ask the banker for feedback and re-do your business proposal accordingly.

If you were to choose B, you would be subscribing to the conventional way of handling failure. For some reason, when we are rejected, we take it as a sign to give up, withdraw from our plans, and return to the normal life we are accustomed to. Remember that succumbing to failure in this manner is a choice and that at any time, you can choose to handle failure as described in options A and C. What I love about option A is that it shows a high level of resilience in the face of rejection. Instead of withdrawing and curling up in a ball of self-pity, option A encourages you to knock on another door and continue knocking until you access an opportunity that's perfect for what you desire to do. I also love option C because it shows a high level of self-discipline in the face of rejection. It takes a lot of humility and self-control to hear someone criticize your goals, and still find ways to learn from them and take on their feedback with grace.

Explosive Step #3

The worst thing you can do after experiencing failure is to not learn anything from it. What's the point of going through setbacks if they will end up being a waste of time? You can make your failure an asset in your journey by ensuring you learn as much as you can from it. The only way to learn from your failures is to stop trying to defend the actions which caused you to fail. I know how uncomfortable it can be to swallow your pride and take advice from someone else, especially when your plans have failed. However, when you have failed at something, it usually means there were systems or processes in your original plan that didn't work very well. This means you need an outsider who has no emotional attachment to the plan to show you where your mistakes might be. If you remain resilient and self-disciplined, you won't have a problem learning from somebody else, especially someone who has accomplished what you desire to accomplish.

Nevertheless, if you are prideful or too attached to your plan, you may feel as though the feedback you get from others is an attack on who you are or on your goals. It's important not to take your failures personally because everyone who is brave enough to try something new will always experience failure along the way. Just because you have failed doesn't mean you are defined by your failure. It also doesn't mean people are judging or mocking you because you have failed. Remind yourself during periods of failure that you are still worthy of success and your failure is only temporary. You will get back in the game armed with new weapons and a new level of determination.

Albert Einstein once said, "Everybody is a genius. But if you judge a fish by its ability to climb a tree, it will live its whole life believing that it is stupid." All of us have a list of strengths and weaknesses. When we compare our weaknesses to other people's strengths, we can easily become discouraged when we fail. For instance, I can pick up a paintbrush, dip it in paint, and move it along a canvas, but I wouldn't say I have the painting skills of Picasso. However, with analytics and numbers, I can come toe-to-toe with the best in my field. If someone who had very little experience with statistics tried to do what I do on an average day, they would fail dismally. This doesn't mean they aren't good at anything; it only means statistics aren't their strong point.

So many times we get caught up in studying the success of people who have completely different strengths and weaknesses than us. Warren Buffett is an exceptional investor who has studied finance and spent much of his time learning about money and how to multiply it. If someone who hasn't invested as much time and money in stocks tried to replicate the investment decisions Buffet has made over time, they would get very different results. This is because Buffet knew exactly when and how much to invest in particular stocks, based on his years of experience, which has made his shares profitable over time. The strategies he has used may not be as effective now because the markets continuously behave differently. Therefore, someone who is inexperienced in investments who wants to become the next Warren Buffett has a very slim chance of doing so because they don't have the same skill set and investment mentality as Buffet.

You are less likely to fail at something you are naturally good at because your mind is a lot more focused on plans you genuinely are passionate about. Think about it: How many hours can you speak about topics you're interested in? In those hours spent speaking about your interests, your brain is stimulated, information flows effortlessly, and your creative mind is awakened. Imagine how productive you would be working in a field that you really loved. You might love the field so much that you open your own business so you can spend a lot more time mastering your knowledge about the field. Even if you were to fail at something you loved, you would have a greater chance of picking yourself up than if you failed at something you weren't really passionate about. Thus, pursuing the plans and goals that set your heart on fire will make failure less offensive and feel like a stumbling block rather than a road closure.

Unfortunately, I cannot give you any tips on how to prevent failure from occurring because I can guarantee you that failure will knock on your door at some point in your life, especially when you decide to pursue your goals or take on a new opportunity. However, I can give you three tips on how to embrace failure and ensure you make the most of it for the short time it is around.

1. Remain Humble

When you are succeeding in life, you can feel as though you are invincible. Your plans may be going well and people may be willing to help you. It's a good feeling to feel like you're on top of the world, and everyone deserves to experience that feeling at least once in their lifetime. However, when failure hits, it can damage your ego, particularly when your ego has been built on succeeding at everything you do. Failure can knock your ego down so badly, it may be difficult to bounce back. Remaining humble will cushion your fall after experiencing failure. Humility reminds you that you are only human and there are so many things out of your control, regardless of how much status or money you have. Humility will also teach you how to be happy during both your highs and lows and how to find happiness in life, outside of your external pursuits.

2. Learn from Your Mistakes

Mistakes aren't a form of punishment from God or a sign you aren't supposed to be pursuing your particular plan. Even the world's wealthiest people have made countless mistakes in their journey to success. The best way to handle failure is by learning from your mistakes. Start asking questions to find out what happened to cause your plans to fail. Was it an error on your part? Was the plan missing some details? Was it an error caused by the people you were working with? Or was it an error no one had control over? Once again, asking specific people for feedback will help you gather more information about your mistakes and see the situation from an outsider's perspective. Don't be afraid to be accountable for your mistakes and accept that you didn't know any better.

3. Embrace Change

Change can be fearful to many people. It's not easy to commit to walking into something you have never experienced before. However, change can also be the best thing to happen to you. It can expose you to another way of looking at life, which can inspire you to grow as an individual. Change can also challenge your idea of a normal life. You may not feel ready to take on an opportunity, but what if that opportunity can usher you into a more fulfilling life's journey? You will only know if change is worthwhile by embracing it and being open to the ways in which you are encouraged to grow and push yourself.

EXPLOSIVE STEP #4

KICKSTARTING A MEANINGFUL LIFE

"The reason we struggle with insecurity is because we compare our behind-the-scenes with everyone else's highlight reel."

— Steven Furtick

There's a natural process that many men and women go through as they grow up. Usually, the process begins with seeking financial stability and ensuring

Explosive Step #4

they have a decent job to fund their lifestyle. Once that has been taken care of, the next step is to move out of their childhood home and mark their own territory. This step can be a lot of fun because, for the first time in their lives, young men and women get to experience what it's like to carry responsibility for themselves and provide their own security. After establishing financial stability and having a taste of freedom, the next step for many young men and women is to seek a partner.

Not everybody cares to have a partner, but I know of many people whose definition of a meaningful life includes having a life partner. I remember when I had reached this step in my natural evolution process, where I was ready to look for someone. Once again, anxiety came knocking on my door, this time with a completely different fear. My fear wasn't that I wouldn't meet a beautiful and smart young woman, but whether they would find me attractive, intelligent, or at least funny! Let's face it, both men and women desire to make the best first impression when meeting each other for the first time.

After several dates (and many lessons learned), I realized the idea of the first impression is a whole lot of hogwash! The truth is, the kind of connection I was looking for required me to be deeply honest with myself and the other person. I couldn't wear any disguises or pretend to be someone I wasn't, otherwise, I wouldn't develop the kind of authentic connection that's worthwhile. I'm convinced if more dating coaches told their clients to simply be themselves to find a partner, they would lose a lot of business. The sad part is being yourself is probably the best way to meet decent people and have decent conversations that can turn into meaningful connections.

Not only did this wisdom empower me in the dating scene, but I could also apply it in my work and personal relationships. Showing up as me, without any masks, was the only way I could live a life free from seeking validation from others or preoccupying myself with what others think of me. Yes, moving away from home and becoming financially stable offers you freedom, but nothing compares to the freedom one gets from learning how to become comfortable in their own skin and feeling like they are living an authentic experience.

— Cece

DON'T BE BOTHERED WITH WHAT PEOPLE THINK OF YOU

It took me many years to understand the value of not being bothered by what others thought about me. From a tender age, I struggled with anxiety, and the only way to calm myself was to avoid any kind of controversy. I would always agree with people, even when I internally disagreed with them. I couldn't imagine openly expressing my views because I was afraid of the back-and-forth confrontation (or at least that's how it felt). Thank goodness I grew up and grew out of my anxiety because, in my adulthood, I am more encouraged to speak my mind and own who I am.

I'll tell you two truths that helped me gain the confidence to not be bothered by what others thought. The first one is simple: It's impossible to make everybody happy. People who suffer from anxiety can easily feel responsible for other people's emotional states. For instance, if someone with anxiety were to express an opinion that made another person upset, they would feel as though they are responsible for making the receiver upset. Is this true though? Can anyone influence how another person chooses to respond? Of course not. Every person is responsible for how they perceive a situation and subsequently, how they react to that situation. If what someone says makes another person upset, the issue lies in how the upset person chose to perceive what was being said (it may have triggered an emotional event or flashback from the past). Therefore, it's really important for those seeking to work through their anxiety to understand they are not responsible for other people's emotional reactions. Although, that doesn't give you a license to go on a rampage, hurting people with your words.

The second truth is this: Not everybody is going to like you. Once again, this is a difficult truth for someone suffering from anxiety to process. Naturally, human beings desire a sense of belonging to a group or community because it secures our survival. However, someone with anxiety is more self-conscious of how others perceive them, and can often take it personally when people openly reject them or seem disinterested in hanging out with them. For instance, a person with anxiety will perceive a text like "Sorry, I cannot see you today" as being a casual way of saying "I don't really want to hang out with you today." Another example is how a person with anxiety may put on a disguise of being a social butterfly so they can have a large circle of friends, even though in the midst of those social gatherings, they are feeling very uncomfortable or triggered.

While it's human nature to want to be liked by others, it can also make you care more about what others think of you than what you think about yourself. In the past, I was guilty of putting my hobbies to the side and engaging in activities my friends were interested in because I felt as though connecting with them was more important than connecting with myself. If I had continued on that road (putting other people before me), I probably would've completely disconnected from who I am, which could have had negative effects on my life.

Lao Tzu has a famous quote that says, "Care about what other people think and you will always be their prisoner." When you care about what other people think of you, you will always be at their mercy. They will manipulate your emotions by purposefully saying hurtful things about you to make you doubt your personal power and destiny. If you have been caught in someone else's prison because of caring too much about what they think of you, here are 10 reasons why you *shouldn't* care what they think:

1. Your Life is Your Own

No one is entitled to your life but you! It doesn't matter how close you are to certain people, your life choices are still 100% yours to make. It's important to know when to lean on others and when it's more appropriate to stand on your own to make serious decisions that will impact your future.

2. No One Knows What's Best for You Better Than Yourself

No one can tap into your heart better than you can. Your goals are extremely personal and they are connected to your life's purpose. This is an experience people cannot relate to because they don't know what it feels like to live in your body or think your thoughts. Of course, there may be friends or family who have been with you for many years and have a good understanding of what you like or dislike, however, even they cannot connect to your soul as deeply as you can.

3. What Someone Else Might Like May Be Wrong for You

Other people's preferences or desires may not be what you want for your life. Many parents are guilty of pressuring their children to study certain skills or pursue certain careers, but how does that usually turn out? The children rebel and end up going in the completely opposite direction. Remember to take a moment to pause and think to yourself, "Is this what I want? Does this decision honor my beliefs and my wishes?"

4. Your Progress Will be Delayed

Concerning yourself about what other people think can cause delays in pursuing your goals or tapping into what you want for yourself. Many times, people's opinions or judgments can cloud our thinking, and for a brief moment, we can be convinced that their opinions are what's good for us. Whenever you receive advice from someone, write it down somewhere and refer back to it later on when you are feeling more level-headed. If you still agree with their advice, you can go ahead and implement it.

5. You're the Only One Who Has to Live With the Consequences

What do you think social media trolls do after they have posted a nasty comment about a celebrity? They simply log off from their social media and continue their daily routine as though nothing happened. How do you think the celebrity reading the comment feels? Their entire day may be ruined, or it may trigger some of their existing insecurities. The moral of the story is that those who criticize or mock you never have any consequences to deal with once they have made their point. You can avoid hurting your feelings by disengaging with them and showing them you don't care about what they have to say. If you have made a public mistake, remind yourself of the acronym F.A.I.L and prepare for your comeback!

6. People Forget What They Say All of the Time

Have you ever held a grudge with somebody who forgot what they said to hurt your feelings? It's anti-climatic, right? I remember a long time ago, during my high school years, being upset with a student about the offensive language they used to address me. I decided to give them the silent treatment, and months went by without us communicating. Eventually, I decided to confront them and tell them how hurt I felt months ago when they used offensive language to address me. The student looked at me with a puzzled face and said, "Are you sure I said that? Because I don't remember." Many times people say things impulsively without thinking it through in their minds. This is why they cannot remember something that probably struck a chord with you.

7. Life is Too Short to Care

You only have one life to live. Are you honestly going to spend your life concerning yourself about what another person thinks? Instead of placing your focus outward and worrying about what other people are saying about you, direct your focus inward, and develop self-awareness. Learn about who you are, what you like and dislike, what your strengths and weaknesses are, and what you desire out of your life.

8. You Become What You Think

When you preoccupy your mind with negativity, you end up manifesting negativity in your life. If you are always thinking about the negative things people may or may not be saying about you, soon enough you will embody these things. Moreover, if you are always thinking about how much people dislike you, you will develop a negative aura or energy, and people will naturally distance themselves from you. Focus instead on the positive qualities you desire people to speak about you. Imagine them saying kind words about you and telling others how much they appreciate you. Imagine yourself being a magnet for positive people and having a strong support system.

9. No One Is Ever Thinking About You as Much as You Think

No one has time to think about you as much as you think. Everyone is going about their business focused on matters involving them. Even if your name comes up in conversation, it's never carried for a long time. The truth is, no one's attention span is strong enough to focus on one person for a long period of time. Thus, you can rest assured knowing that no grown adult with a life has enough time to talk about you all the time.

10. Some People Will Never Be Satisfied

There are some people you can never please with your actions, no matter how hard you try. Even when you meet their expectations, they will often find a reason to discredit your hard work or efforts. For instance, if you prepare a meal for them they will say, "The food is too salty," and when you reduce the

Explosive Step #4

amount of salt in the food they will say, "The food is too bland." It's important to identify people like this in your friendship circles and family so you don't exert all of your energy trying to please people who will never be satisfied.

FORGIVE YOURSELF FOR YOUR PAST MISTAKES

We've all done things or spoken words we weren't proud of. Maybe you had pretty wild partying days and strained your relationships because of it, or maybe you haven't always been a pro at saving money, and you would frequently have to borrow money from others. If we had to discuss all of the embarrassing and hurtful things we have done in our past, we would simply depress ourselves. There will never be an appropriate time to dwell on the past because it has come and gone. All of our "should haves" and "could haves" aren't helpful when we're seeking a better life for ourselves, because we can't go back and redo our pasts.

Part of the process of healing from past hurts is to forgive people who may have caused us pain. However, how many times do we add our own names to the list of people who have caused us pain? It seems quite bizarre to think that we participated in causing a lot of drama in our lives. Usually, we would pass the blame to someone else and make them responsible for the dark times we endured. Although many times, we also need to take responsibility for the decisions we chose which brought about negative consequences that either we or those around us, had to suffer with.

Take a moment and think back to a really wild or difficult time in your life where you were a part of a lot of drama in your environment. It may have been drama in your household, drama at work, or drama in your friendship circles. You may not have caused the drama, but think back to what you did

Explosive Step #4

or didn't do in the situation. Did you watch as one of your friends got bullied? Did you perhaps misuse your parents' money and lie about what you spent it on? Did you get a hold of an exam answer sheet before the exam took place and peek at the answers? If you think long and hard enough, you will recall a number of incidents where you didn't use good judgment, or you made decisions that hurt yourself or other people.

It's time to forgive yourself for the many times you thought you were doing something right but instead created a lot of suffering for yourself. It's time for you to forgive yourself for your emotional outbursts which may have deeply hurt those you love. The truth is no one is without sin. All of us make mistakes and react impulsively at times. Forgiving yourself isn't an easy process, but it's one that can set you free and remove the heavy burden off your shoulders. It may be hard for you to forgive yourself because you think no one would ever forgive you if they knew some of the things you have done. But quite frankly, if some of your friends and family were to open up, you would find they have a dark past too.

One of the hindrances to self-forgiveness is remaining in a state of guilt. You feel guilty because you acted in ways you consider shameful or did things your family wouldn't be proud of. The heavy guilt causes you to walk with your head down and eats away at your self-confidence. In some cases, people may use this guilt as a form of self-punishment or self-sabotage. When getting to know new people, you might carry yourself like a broken person or try to convince your new acquaintances that you are pathetic and not worth getting to know.

The consequences of carrying guilt from your past mistakes can have long-term consequences too. For instance, since you feel worthless or have low self-esteem, you may be drawn to people who are also feeling broken and have low self-esteem. You may also engage in low-value activities like binge drinking or getting high the

Explosive Step #4

whole day with no hopes of getting up and doing something with your life. Back when I was frustrated with constant job rejections, I turned to alcohol and drugs to escape the pressure I was in. I was ashamed of hanging out with some of my friends who were doing well for themselves, because quite frankly, I thought I wasn't good enough to hang out with them. Instead, I found friends who were also seeking an escape through substances like me. These were my party friends who were always available when it was time to go out and dance the night away. When I finally got my act together, my party friends somehow disappeared. Our priorities didn't align any longer. I lost contact with them, but to be honest, I also outgrew that wild phase of my life.

When you decide to forgive yourself for past mistakes, you will see your life differently. No longer will you engage in self-destructive behaviors or speak down about yourself. Instead, you will crave new and healthy experiences and look for friends who can mirror the positivity you feel inside. The type of partners you attract romantically will change too. You will begin attracting partners who desire healing and self-improvement just as much as you do.

Forgiving yourself requires you to come face-to-face with the periods of your life you would much rather forget and acknowledge that they actually happened. Try and recall as many memories as you can which occurred during that period, and sit with the feelings those memories conjure up. When reflecting on the dark times of your life, it's important to remember not to judge yourself or be heavily critical. You may have outgrown that phase of your life, however, back then you didn't know as much as you know now. If you feel the need to become judgmental, focus on how much love you needed back then. Show yourself the love, understanding, and compassion you were searching for in harmful people, places, or things.

Here are three strategies you can implement when working on self-forgiveness:

1. Categorize the Offense

Many offenses are forgivable, but generally speaking, people have a hard time forgiving themselves for the following offenses:

- Failing at a major life task, like making a marriage work, or becoming financially independent.
- When your actions cause a lot of pain for another person.
- When you have hurt yourself through destructive habits like drinking or infidelity.
- When you have lied about doing something really important, like saving money toward your children's education or telling your family that you go to work every day even though you were actually fired.

Categorizing the offense requires you to look at what you feel guilty for and name it. For instance, instead of saying "I feel guilty for being a bad mother," you would think about the root cause of your guilt and express how you feel you have wronged your family.

2. Know How You Feel

Once you have categorized the offense, you will have a better understanding of what has been eating away at you for so long. The next step is to associate emotions with the offense you have committed. For example, if your temper caused a breakdown in your relationships, you may associate hopelessness, loneliness, disappointment, and frustration with the offense. You may have been hopeless because you didn't understand how to subdue your anger, lonely because none of your friends knew how to help you, disappointed at how your temper ruined your relationships and frustrated with yourself for not being a better person at the time.

3. Understand What You Want Going Forward

Perhaps you don't want to reconcile with the people you hurt in the past, but you want to release the guilt and shame you have been carrying around with you for years. Getting closure doesn't require you to make contact with people from the past and apologize, however, if you feel like that is what will bring you closure, you can. Remember the focus here is about forgiving yourself and setting your soul free. Write yourself a letter and express that you forgive yourself for all of the offenses you have made in the past. Show yourself compassion and put the past to rest. If you desire to implement new goals in your life, write these goals down on a piece of paper and hang the paper in a place you can regularly see it. Hold yourself accountable to the new goals you desire to incorporate into your life and celebrate every small victory.

Explosive Step #4

BUILD A STRONG SUPPORT SYSTEM

As "safe" as you might feel cooped up at home alone, you would be a happier person if you had a strong support system. A support system is a network of people, which may include your friends, family members, colleagues, church friends, or members of your community. You don't need to be extremely close with someone for them to be a part of your network of support, although they need to provide a distinct value in your life. For instance, the colleague you can turn to whenever you are having trouble with a particular application may not be your friend, but they are an asset in your career growth.

Studies have shown there are many benefits of having a strong and healthy support system in your life. For instance, those with strong support systems have been found to have a higher well-being and live much longer (Butler, L., n.d.) This is because your support network can make you more resilient in facing obstacles and managing stress. In addition to helping you manage stress, your support system can help you identify stressors in your environment and help you think of ways to destress or cut back on the number of tasks you perform on a daily basis.

Having a support system can also help you succeed in life. Your network of support can help you find a job or plan your career development. They can transfer skills, share information with you, and offer guidance when you have to make important decisions about your life. This component of a support system can bring you a lot of comfort, especially when you are feeling insecure in your life.

If you desire a strong support system, you need to feel comfortable letting other people into your life. You can always control how much or how little you share with your network, but in order for them to provide guidance and emotional support, they will need to know a little bit about what you are going through or where your anxiety stems from. Therefore, I believe it's crucial you build a level of trust with each person you intend on adding to your support system. If you don't feel like you can trust someone, they may not be the best person to include in your network. It's also important to only include people you can depend on. Think about each person you intend on including in your network, and ask yourself if you feel comfortable calling them in the middle of the night. Do you think that person would be dependable in your time of need? If your answer is

Explosive Step #4

yes, they may be a good fit for your network.

Once you have come up with a list of people to include in your network, you need to assess whether you can show up for them in their time of need. Successful support systems have a good balance of give-and-take, so before you can require anything from them, you will need to ensure you can offer the same amount of support they give to you.

Here are a few ways you can maintain your support system once you have formed one:

- **Show your appreciation.** Remind your friends how much they mean to you whenever you get an opportunity to. If you appreciate something they did for you, make a point to express your gratitude by saying "Thank you."
- **Stay in touch.** If you miss your friends or family, drop them a text or call them to find out how they are doing. Don't forget

birthdays or any other special occasion in their lives; special occasions may also be a good opportunity to remind them how much they mean to you.
- **Show up for them whenever they need you.** If your friend wants to speak to you about something, make time to listen to them. If they are going through a hard time, go over to their house and spend some time with them.
- **Cheer them on.** When someone in your support system achieves a goal, be the first one to congratulate them. Celebrate their successes with them, and let them know how proud you are of them.
- **Accept assistance.** It can be difficult to accept help from people, but your support system will want to feel like they have done something to make your life better, especially when you are feeling low. If a friend offers to come and visit you, make time to see them, even if it's for a few

minutes. Accepting help from your support system will also keep the relationship between you balanced.

HAVING A SUPPORTIVE PARTNER

If you are old enough to date, you might want to consider having a supportive intimate partner. Not every romantic partner you will be with will be supportive, thus you need to be careful when choosing the right one. Ideally, a supportive partner creates a safe space for you to share your thoughts and feelings, without feeling like you are being judged. They are also good at encouraging you to voice your concerns and showing you affection when you're feeling low.

Similar to the support system, it's important to strike a good balance between give-and-take in your romantic relationship. The last thing you want is for your partner to feel like you are depending on them too much or vice versa. Remember, even if your partner seems independent and in control of their feelings, they also desire support from you, and to feel as though you have their back as much as they have yours. It's also good to remember that even though your partner always has the best advice or can make you feel really good about yourself, you are the only one who can make yourself happy (remember that you are responsible for your own emotions).

You need to commit to making yourself happy, and your partner can come in and enhance the positive emotions you already feel. If you are going through a difficult time, it may be healthier for you to see a counselor instead of relying on your partner to help you address some of the strong emotional triggers you are experiencing. If you want, you can ask your partner to join you in some of your counseling sessions so they get an understanding of the kind of personal issues you are dealing with.

Supportive partners can hold space for you while you address certain issues in your life, however, they aren't people who will agree with every emotion or behavior you exhibit. If your partner has a high level of self-respect, they will not tolerate any kind of bullying behavior, all in the name of "being supportive." Supportive partners will challenge you to look at the world differently, get out of your own head, and consider stepping out of your comfort zone. They won't wallow in self-pity with you or validate your insecurities just because it's something you want to hear. Their job is to stand beside you and encourage you to overcome your fears.

EXPLOSIVE STEP #5

INTENSIFYING WORKOUTS

WITH BRAIN FOOD

"Exercise is king. Nutrition is queen. Put them together and you've got a kingdom."

— Jack LaLanne

I once had a friend who was a living, breathing genius. I thought he would be perfect in the world of coding and analytics, but he preferred the world of business. This man was so convincing when he spoke,

Explosive Step #5

he could sell a dollar pen for hundreds of bucks. I would spend weekends at his house, listening to the many business ideas he had that could change society.

After a while, I realized my friend was a good talker but poor at executing his plans. He could pitch a million-dollar business in less than 20 minutes, but when I would ask him how far he was in implementing the idea, he would come up with several excuses. "I'm still waiting for the licenses to be approved" he'd say, or, "I'm refining the marketing strategy, I'll be launching soon." I would wait a few months and return to my friend with the same question: How far are you in implementing the idea? Once more, he would give me excuses, each time he had completely new reasons for the delays.

I got to a point of being frustrated with him. I could tell he was a gifted person, but for some reason, he wasn't able to use his gifts appropriately. He desired to be successful, but most of the time, his desires remained fantasies. I began thinking of ways to gently encourage him to at least take the first step. I knew he would get defensive if I pointed out his poor execution skills, so instead, I challenged him with a fitness plan. He wasn't the fittest guy in the world, and neither was I, but I knew he was extremely competitive and would be interested in taking up my offer.

The challenge was simple: Who can grow the biggest muscles in six months? There weren't any restrictions on the methods we could use to grow our muscles, except for the fact that we couldn't use any steroids in the process. The muscle had to be gained naturally, through a rigorous fitness routine carried out across several months. When the six months were up, my friend had grown three times the muscles I had built, although I knew this would be the case. The impressive part is that during the six months, he made more progress on his business idea than he had ever made since its inception. By committing to exercising—a goal that seemed unrelated to his entrepreneurial success—he could carry the same level of discipline into other areas of his life. Thus, the stronger he got physically, the sharper he became mentally.

— *Veejay*

THE CONNECTION BETWEEN MENTAL HEALTH AND WORKING OUT

You probably know how beneficial working out is for your body, but did you know it's also great for improving your overall mental health? Many times, people start working out because of their desire to lose weight or gain muscle, but after achieving their dream body, they start to slack on their workouts. The mental health benefits of physical exercise are still misunderstood and as a result, many people are missing out on an effective way of keeping their mental health in check.

Just by exercising two to three times per week, you could experience an improvement in your sleep pattern, have a sharper memory, and feel more positive about yourself and your current life situation. I mean, who wouldn't want to experience these benefits? What's even better is there aren't any specific exercises that are better than others when it comes to improving your mental well-being. Even a relaxed 30-minute walk twice a week or a 30-minute dance lesson can help you feel lighter and happier about your life.

Exercise and Depression

There have been studies that have shown how physical exercise can treat mild-to-moderate depression just as well as antidepressants can (without the side effects that can come with an antidepressant). For example, a study conducted by the Harvard T.H. Chan School of Public Health showed how running for 15 minutes each day or going on a relaxing walk for an hour can reduce the risk of depression by 26%

(Robinson, L. et al., 2020). Physical exercise is seen to be a superpower in the fight against depression because it promotes a chemical change in the brain, reduces inflammation, promotes neural growth, and releases feel-good hormones that improve your psychological state of mind.

Exercise and Anxiety

Similar to how physical exercise can work as a natural antidepressant, exercise can also be a wonderful anti-anxiety treatment (once again, without the many side effects that come with anti-anxiety drugs). After a workout session, your energy will usually increase, you will feel less tension in your body, and the heavy thoughts on your mind will often disappear (sometimes even during the workout). Think of exercise as going on a mental holiday for 30 minutes to an hour where you can have a safe and healthy escape from your thoughts and give your mind and body time to relax.

Exercise and Stress

Have you ever noticed how tense your body feels when you are overly stressed? You may feel your neck and shoulder muscles tighten, leaving you with neck and back pain. You might also experience severe headaches which can blur your vision or cause you to lose concentration. In some cases, stress can even cause you to lose sleep, or disturb your sleeping patterns, and make you feel grumpy or highly sensitive at work and home. Physical exercise can reduce the symptoms of stress and release endorphins in the brain. This has a similar effect as morphine, helping your body relax, loosen up, and overall feel much healthier.

Explosive Step #5

PLANNING YOUR BEGINNER'S FITNESS ROUTINE

You don't need to commit hours out of your day to exercise. When it comes to working out, a little done consistently goes a long way. In the beginning, you can aim to work out three days a week. Remember to always start with moderate exercises and build up to more intense exercises. For instance, in the first week, you could dedicate 10 minutes, three times a week, to playing physical workout games online or on a Nintendo Wii, or going outside for a brief walk. Your goal during the first week should be to raise your heart rate and break a small sweat. Take as many short breaks as you need and make sure you're staying hydrated throughout your workout session.

In week two, you will increase the duration of your workouts to 20 minutes, three times a week. At this point, your body will have a lot more energy to exert during workout sessions. Increase the intensity of your workouts, depending on your fitness level. For example, you could do a combination of squats, push-ups, burpees, and lunges. If you're not a fan of traditional exercises, you can spend 20 minutes watching an aerobics video or dancing to your favorite high-tempo tunes. I always recommend you spend your workouts doing exercises you genuinely love so that your brain can associate working out with a pleasurable activity.

Explosive Step #5

On weeks three and four, you can increase the duration of your workout sessions to 30 minutes and spend a good portion of that time outdoors. The great thing about exercising outdoors is you can break a sweat while connecting with nature and subsequently feel more grounded. Go on a run around the local park or ride your bicycle around the neighborhood. When you get back home, you can end off your session with ground exercises, like sit-ups and leg raises, and a long stretch. When exercising outdoors, remember to pack a bottle of water to stay hydrated and a snack (in case you feel light-headed and need a boost of energy). After four weeks of building up your stamina and workout intensity, you can either maintain the same intensity as weeks three and four or intensify your workouts. Intense workouts that raise the heart rate for longer periods make you comfortable with such feelings even after the workout.

If you're looking to intensify your workouts, you will need to engage in high-intensity interval training (HIIT) workouts. There are so many HIIT workout videos on YouTube for you to scroll through to find a routine you may be interested in trying. Local gyms usually have great HIIT programs you can sign up for, along with other classes which include weight training and kickboxing. Studies have shown that exercise training programs which are 30 minutes each, and last no more than 12 weeks, have resulted in a huge improvement in anxiety (Herring, 2010).

Even after detailing a beginner's fitness routine, I know there will be some people who need an extra push. We all know how important physical exercise is for us, but many times it's difficult to feel motivated to put on our workout clothes and simply do it! If you need an extra push, try asking a friend to join you in your workout sessions. Having a gym buddy or joining a club can add a social element to working out, which can provide you with the encouragement you need. Besides needing motivation, there can also be other barriers that get in the way of you committing to your workouts.

The following are three of the most common barriers and how to overcome them:

1. "Work was hectic, I want to go home and take a nap!"

You might wake up early in the morning and be too tired, or come home from work and your body isn't in the mood to workout. You feel exhausted, and the last thing you want to do is run on a treadmill and exert what's remaining of your energy. Ironically, exercising when you're tired may be the best way to energize your body. During and after a workout, your body burns fat for fuel, and this releases a lot of energy. When you're feeling tired, commit to a quick and fun workout. Chances are your energy levels will increase during the workout and you could train for even longer than you intended.

2. "I have so much to do. I think I'll skip my workout today."

When you have a lot on your mind, working out may be the last task on your priority list (if you even remember it's on there). This is especially true when you have a lot of roles to juggle, like being a working, single mother and having to get home to prepare dinner for your family. The thought of going to the gym can seem overwhelming. The best way to get out of this "funk" is to start thinking of exercise as one of your main priorities. You don't think twice about going to work five days a week or making a trip to the grocery store to stock up on food. Likewise, exercise should become a permanent part of your day—a non-negotiable of some sort. You don't have to necessarily commit to a specific type of exercise, but you do have to move your body and break a sweat for a few minutes each week.

3. "I'm self-conscious of my body!"

As much as many people desire to workout, there are some who may feel

Explosive Step #5

discouraged because of their negative body image. Going to a local gym may cause them to feel embarrassed, especially if they perceive themselves as being overweight or looking unattractive in gym clothing. If you are feeling self-conscious about your body, you can ask a friend to exercise with you so your mind isn't focused on what everybody else is doing at the gym. You could even take your workouts outdoors, choosing the least busy time to go on a walk or ride a bicycle. Finally, there are so many workouts you can do right from the comfort of your home! However, I would also recommend seeing a counselor to help you work through your body image issues because ultimately, these issues don't go away after you have lost weight or gained muscle—they are rooted in your mind.

Explosive Step #5

LOAD UP ON BRAIN FOOD

Food is supposed to be a source of fuel to help your body move and maintain good health. However, how many times have we (and I must include myself) gone on a binge eating episode to numb how we feel or reward ourselves for good behavior? My specific go-to foods when I'm feeling low are french fries, a juicy burger, and chocolate ice cream. None of these foods are good sources of fuel for my body; instead, they make me feel full, lethargic, and full of other cravings!

There are certain foods that are good for your body and others that are good for your brain. Yes, that's right. Certain foods you find in the grocery store can boost your memory and improve your mental health. When your brain wants to store, access, or transmit memories, it uses chemical messengers known as neurotransmitters (Morris, 2017). To produce neurotransmitters, the brain needs to extract nutrients from specific foods. If your diet consists of sugary, high-carb foods, your brain won't be able to produce neurotransmitters, which in the long term may result in memory loss.

So, what are the nutrients your brain needs for optimal brain health?

1. Iron

A study published in the American Journal of Clinical Nutrition showed how women with sufficient levels of iron could answer test questions incredibly faster and more accurately than women with an iron deficiency (Morris, 2017). The study also found that when the women with an iron deficiency were given 16 weeks of iron supplementation, their test scores improved seven-fold. Add iron-rich foods to your diet, such as red meat, spinach, and pumpkin seeds.

2. Choline

Choline is one of the essential nutrients used to produce neurotransmitters and has also been seen to boost concentration and memory. A study looking at healthy seniors aged between 50- and 80-years found that when the seniors were given two tablespoons of choline-rich lecithin every day, their memory improved significantly, and after five weeks, memory lapses reduced by 48% (Morris, 2017). Some foods that are rich in choline include fish, eggs, seeds, soybeans, and nuts.

3. Folate

Folate is found predominantly in leafy vegetables and fruit. Folate deficiency is a known cause of memory loss. Not only does folate aid in good brain health, but it also improves red blood cell formation and function, and helps balance depressive moods. Some of the best foods which contain folate include broccoli, strawberries, asparagus, and bran cereals.

4. Glucose

Glucose makes up 20% of your body's fuel source. This means your diet must include a significant amount of glucose to ensure your brain is functioning optimally. The best source of glucose is carbohydrates, and including them in each meal will ensure your body has plenty of glucose to feed to your brain. Since your brain cannot store glucose, it needs a constant supply of it throughout the day. Therefore, break up your meals and snack in between larger meals to supply your brain with a consistent amount of glucose every day.

5. Water

Oh, how we can forget water—the miracle drink we love to ignore! Your body needs liquids to transport nutrients to the brain. Drinking plenty of water helps to move nutrients to your brain and keep your body functioning effectively. Going hours or days without drinking clean water can lead to dehydration, which can leave you feeling fatigued and interfere with your cognitive abilities. If you are put off by the taste of water, dice up some fruit to give it added flavor. You can also eat foods with high water content, like tomatoes, watermelon, grapefruit, cucumber, broccoli, and celery.

THREE HARMFUL EATING HABITS TO BREAK NOW

What causes people to overeat? Is it a lack of willpower or using food to numb how they feel? The truth is that people overeat for many reasons, and sometimes the reason is as simple as them developing harmful eating habits. Habits can be very difficult to break since your brain has already learned the behavior and probably performs it automatically. For example, it may be a habit for you to drink a cup of coffee in the morning and only eat your first meal of the day during your lunch break, or maybe you are used to driving past your favorite takeaway spot after work to grab dinner. Getting a grip on your harmful eating habits requires you to first become aware of them.

Explosive Step #5

Here are three eating habits you need to break NOW:

1. Mindless Eating

When you're watching TV, do you find yourself reaching for snacks in your cupboard? Mindless eating can contribute to weight gain because you continue to eat even when you're not hungry. You may be triggered to eat by environmental situations, like catching up on your favorite series, going out for drinks with friends, or ordering food at the movies.

Cravings can also trigger mindless eating. For instance, you see a commercial for your favorite meal at a takeaway spot you frequent and your mind develops a craving. Thirty minutes later, you find yourself holding said meal in your hands because you felt compelled to satisfy your craving. The best way to avoid mindless eating is to take a moment and connect with your body. Are you hungry? Peckish? Full? Before eating, it's also good to drink water because sometimes symptoms of dehydration, like having a dry mouth, may come across as symptoms of hunger.

2. Skipping Breakfast

Are you really not hungry at breakfast, or is your mind simply trained not to eat breakfast? The reason breakfast is the most important meal of the day is because it breaks the fast (see what I did there?). Think about it for a moment. The average dinner time in America is between 6:00 p.m. and 7:30 p.m. If you wake up at 6:00 a.m. to get ready for work, you would have gone without food for about 12 hours. Now, let's say you grab a coffee because you're not hungry and you want to beat the traffic going to work. Coffee will suppress your appetite and your next meal may be around lunchtime. How many hours of fasting would that be? And where is your body supposed to get energy from to sustain you during the day?

Skipping breakfast not only affects your energy levels but it can also slow down your metabolism, which over time can lead to serious health issues, such as obesity. To ensure you eat breakfast, consciously make a point of preparing healthy breakfast options the night before so in the morning you will have enough time to enjoy your meal. Healthy breakfast options include muesli and yogurt, eggs and avocado on toasted bread, or vegetable juices and fruit smoothies.

3. Emotional Eating and Binge Drinking

You have a horrible day at the office, and as you rush out of the building, you think of passing the grocery store and picking up the biggest tub of ice cream, or ordering a large pizza for one. For many people, food is the best distraction when there's a lot to mentally or emotionally process. Instead of working through the mental clutter, people find it relaxing to enjoy flavorful food and focus instead on how good the food makes them feel. Besides food, others may turn to alcohol as a way of numbing their emotions. According to the Centers for Disease Control and Prevention, excessive drinking (also known as binge drinking) constitutes as four or more drinks during a single occasion for women and five or more drinks during a single occasion for men (Centers for Disease Control and Prevention, 2020). Healthier coping mechanisms you can implement to avoid emotional eating or binge drinking include journaling, speaking to a trusted friend or counselor, or adopting a spiritual practice, like prayer or meditation. Refer to Part 1 of this book to learn how to identify your anxiety triggers.

EXPLOSIVE STEP #6

TRIGGERING THE LAST CHORE

"The mind is a wonderful servant, but a terrible master."

— Robin Sharma

I met a really wonderful person at a mutual friend's birthday party. Her name was Macy, and we seemed to click instantly. One reason we seemed to get along so well was that we were both hovering around the chip table. People with anxiety love to hover around the chip table. Why? Because eating food at a party gives us something to do when we're avoiding socializing with everybody else. After talking about our favorite snacks, the conversation moved to sleep. Macy told me how she hasn't had a good night's rest for weeks.

At first, I thought it was because she had a stressful job, but it turned out she was struggling with anxiety. She told me that she had always had issues with sleep patterns, but in the last few weeks, her anxiety was skyrocketing because she was having trouble in her romantic relationship. This affected the quality of her sleep. She went from being a deep sleeper to an extremely light sleeper, being woken up by passing cars or creaks in the house during the night. I could tell from the bags under her eyes that she was exhausted!

I suggested she start preparing for bed in the same way she would prepare for work. She would follow a bedtime routine consisting of activities that would calm her mind and body. I checked in with her about a week later and although her sleeping patterns were still irregular, Macy was proud to share that she had several nights where she fell into a deep sleep after following her bedtime routine. From the sound of her voice over the phone, Macy's energy levels were a lot higher than the last time we had met, and she sounded a lot happier too!

— Arielle

HOW ANXIOUS PEOPLE FEEL ABOUT BEDTIME

Anxiety can creep up on you in the morning, during the day, and at night. Quite frankly, it's an intrusive little bugger that sometimes just won't leave you alone! Anxiety in the evenings can be a stressful event since nighttime is usually when your body is supposed to relax and recharge. The primary reason for experiencing anxiety in the evenings is not being able to switch off your mind. You might stare at the ceiling, scroll through your social media, or research a few ideas you had on your mind the entire day.

Anxiety can also be triggered by not feeling safe in your environment. For instance, a creak in the wall or slam of a door can frighten you and interrupt your sleep. You may also feel anxious about an enormous crisis you are dealing with at work or in your relationship, which you can't seem to wrap your head around. If what you're anxious about is within your control, tell yourself you will address it in the morning. However, if what you're anxious about is out of your control, learn to accept the situation for what it is, and let go of trying to figure it out. You can also reach out to your support system and share what's been heavy on your mind. Since they know you so well, they will certainly have a few words of encouragement to share.

How many times have you pleaded with your brain to calm down and give you a few hours of uninterrupted sleep?

The irony in this is that even the thought of not being able to fall asleep can be the reason you're finding it so hard to fall asleep! A lack of sleep can make you feel grouchy in the morning, causing you to have no desire to interact with people or be productive at work. All you're thinking of is going back home, climbing into your bed, and catching up on lost sleep. The short-term consequences of poor sleep are a disturbance in your mood, however, the long-term consequences can prove to be dire. For instance, poor sleep has been associated with heart disease, diabetes, and a weakened immune system (Collins, 2013).

Sleep isn't a luxury, it's a necessity. While you're sleeping, your body is repairing cells, tissues, and muscles, and sorting through your thoughts and emotions. After a good night's rest, you wake up feeling refreshed, as though your mind and body have reset, and you're ready to tackle the new day with new strength. It's recommended you get eight hours of undisturbed sleep because that's how long it takes for your body to fully rest. When you're suffering from anxiety, you're lucky to get in a few hours of sleep. Since your mind and body haven't fully recharged, you typically wake up carrying the same heavy burdens of yesterday on your mind and feel unprepared for the new day.

My personal struggles with poor sleep started when in high school, but grew progressively worse as life became more stressful (and I had to assume a lot more responsibility). I would suffer from unexpected panic attacks during the night, which left me feeling afraid of each coming night. I was caught in an anxiety-perpetuating cycle - every time I would prepare for bed, I would start feeling stressed. My stress would keep me up at night, and this would lead to an anxiety-triggered panic. I wanted to learn my sleep patterns, so I got myself a smartwatch and wore it some nights. The alarm I set on my watch helped me wake up at a set time, which then allowed my body to adapt to a more positive sleep schedule. By waking up at the same time consistently, I began to naturally fall asleep at the same time consistently each night.

HOW TO BEAT NIGHT-TIME ANXIETY AND RECLAIM YOUR BEAUTY SLEEP

The worst-case scenarios seem to plague my mind most at night. Imagine losing sleep because you're thinking about events that haven't even occurred! Those who struggle with nighttime anxiety know how frustrating it can be to be the only person awake at night while the rest of the city is asleep. The best solution for addressing nighttime anxiety is to seek help from a professional mental health practitioner (nothing can beat this suggestion). However, there are five actionable solutions you can implement at home right now to help reduce your anxiety before you go to sleep:

1. Create a Sleep Routine and Get in Bed Around the Same Time

Sleep routines work in the same way as morning routines do. In the morning, your routine may involve taking 20 minutes to reflect on your goals, hopping into the shower, fixing yourself a healthy breakfast, and making your way to work. Your sleep routine would include activities that are stress-relieving so you can relax your mind before going to sleep. What's considered "relaxing" for one person may not fit the category for another, thus, it's important to commit to activities *you* find relaxing and pleasurable. To maximize the full potential of your body clock, you need to maintain consistency in the times you go to sleep and wake up. This will ensure your body naturally goes to sleep and wakes up at certain times. If you watch television until 9:00 p.m., give yourself a period of 30 minutes to get into bed. Make sure your room is dark, and all technology is switched off. Set your alarm to wake you up 30 minutes before your normal waking hour. This will give you a gap of 30 minutes to fully wake up and feel alert. Follow this schedule consistently so it can become part of your natural body clock.

2. Unplug from Electronic Devices

Using electronic devices right until you go to sleep can be what's keeping you awake at night. Let's face it: Technology is addictive, and a quick browse through your social media feed, or a quick Google search, can turn into an hour of exploration. What's surprising is you don't even feel the time that's spent on your device because you're so tuned in to what you're reading or watching. Give yourself a technology curfew where you decide to unplug for the night.

The blue light from electronic device screens may also affect the quality of your sleep. The blue light coming from your laptop, cell phone, or TV screen can stimulate your brain and keep you alert when you're supposed to be asleep. If you're working late at night and you need to continue using your electronic devices, consider purchasing a blue light blocking screen or blue light glasses to protect your brain and your eyes.

Lastly, your anxiety could be caused by something known as doom scrolling. Have you ever heard of what that is? To put it plainly, doom scrolling is the excessive scrolling on the internet and absorbing negativity and bad news (which many times isn't even real). Doom scrolling reached new highs during the global pandemic of 2020. Many people relied on the internet as their main source for information on the latest updates. I know of some people who were constantly checking the increasing death tolls every day. How do you think absorbing that kind of information will make you feel? Scrolling on the internet mindlessly will reinforce negative thoughts and cause you to adopt a pessimistic mindset about your life, the economy, and everything in between. If you're prone to anxiety, I'd recommend you put time limits to your usage of the internet. You can also use in-built apps to limit the time of social media, and disable news alerts and notifications, to avoid having to check on your phone every so often.

3. Building a List Before Bed

Consider journaling or writing your task list before bed. Write down all of your pressing thoughts and feelings so you can feel at ease and hopefully forget them before you sleep. When you can wake up in the morning, and look at all of the tasks, notes, and thoughts you wrote down the night before, you can address them with a fresh mind. This exercise doesn't have to take a long time. Some people will find it enjoyable to write for 30 minutes, however, 5 minutes before you sleep is all you need.

4. Drink Chamomile Tea Before Bed

For many years, people have used chamomile tea as a natural remedy to reduce anxiety and treat insomnia. Many people regard this tea as a mild tranquilizer because of its calming effects and how it promotes sleep. If

Explosive Step #6

you want to induce sleepiness, fix yourself a cup of chamomile tea about 45 minutes to an hour before your bedtime. This will give your body sufficient time to metabolize the tea and allow the natural sedative effects to kick in.

5. Practice a Few De-stressing Visualization Techniques

Have you ever tried a visualization technique? It engages your imagination and helps you create mental images associated with the outcomes you desire to see in your reality. By drawing these mental images, your brain is tricked into believing you are actually experiencing the desired outcome in the present moment. Over time, visualization can reprogram your mind to behave in a manner consistent with your desires. Below is an example of a visualization script for reducing anxiety and slowing down the intensity of your thoughts:

> Lay in your bed in a comfortable position. Make sure your back is supported and feel the weight of

your body gently sink into the bed. When you are ready, you can close your eyes. Take a few deep breaths until you feel a sense of calm.

Visualize a table with filing cabinets underneath it hovering in front of your face. On the table are multiple papers scattered all over, some on top of each other, and others gathered in folders. As you look closely at some of the papers, you find that some have a huge red stamp written "Urgent," and others have a huge green stamp written "Not urgent." Among some of the urgent files are papers related to work projects, papers related to your family affairs, and others related to your health.

Take a few deep breaths, and when you are ready, pick up one piece of paper (it doesn't matter if it is part of the urgent or not urgent category) and store it in an appropriate cabinet

Explosive Step #6

underneath the table. If the piece of paper is an urgent work-related matter, store it in the urgent tasks filing cabinet. If it is a non-urgent work-related matter, store it in the non-urgent tasks filing cabinet.

Visualize yourself sorting through each piece of paper until there are none left on top of the table. As you file each piece of paper, remind yourself you are not discarding the issue, but instead clearing your mind for the night, so you can have a fresh start in the morning and feel more prepared to face your responsibilities head-on. You don't need to panic about forgetting certain information because you have filed every thought under the correct cabinet, making it easy to source at a later time.

EXPLOSIVE STEP #7

BEING PROACTIVE WITH COMMITMENTS

"Unless commitment is made, there are only promises and hopes; but no plans."

— Peter F. Drucker

*I*n 2019, I was involved in severe company politics, which almost cost my job. A number of organizational changes had impacted the course of our team. All the hard work and dedication I had invested in

Explosive Step #7

my career was about to be thrown in the drain. For many months, I stressed about my job security. I would wake up in a panic, go to work in a panic, and sleep in a panic. I felt as though my body was stuck in survival mode, and the powerful adrenaline within me was, at times, too much to bear.

My mental and physical health had deteriorated so much that I didn't have the desire to eat, socialize, or do anything that wasn't work-related. After turning down several invitations to see my friends and family, I had what many people call an "Aha" moment, or divine revelation. I realized I was more committed to listening to my anxiety and letting it overpower me than I was deliberately stepping out of my comfort zone and regaining control over my life. Of course, I couldn't change my work situation because it was out of my control, but I didn't have to be buried in fear because of it!

I wanted to restore the happiness in my life that had been stolen by an outlier event. I wanted to feel like the happy-

go-lucky person who I am and reconnect with my support system. All it took to reduce my anxiety was a choice: I simply wanted something different, and I was going to pursue it, even if it meant pursuing it scared. I wasn't going to wait until my work situation improved before pursuing peace in my life because, quite frankly, we are living on borrowed time. I took small steps each day to restore my sense of well-being, and after a few months, I had reconnected with myself. Did I still feel anxious about my work situation? Yeah, sure! But it didn't paralyze me the same way it used to.

— Deshaun

Explosive Step #7

CREATING AN ACTION PLAN TO DEAL WITH YOUR ANXIETY

Going forward, you will need to have an anxiety action plan to help you address sudden moments of feeling anxious so you don't resort to old behavioral patterns. Having a plan detailing how you will respond to anxiety attacks will also give you a sense of control when you feel as though you're losing your mind. Your anxiety action plan can be the safety blanket you need before committing to new plans or seeking new opportunities. It will remind you how to deal with emotional triggers, such as change, visiting unknown places, or making new friends.

As we've discussed earlier in the book, the world is full of uncertainty. Nevertheless, your anxiety action plan can provide you with comfort during moments of uncertainty. You won't feel the need to escape an uncertain situation because your action plan will have all the tools and reminders you need to confront various life challenges head-on! I've created a four-step process you can use to write down your anxiety action plan. Remember to make several copies of your action plan and keep one in a place you frequently visit, like your bedroom, car, or office desk.

1. Get Specific About Your Worries

When you're anxious, your first thought might be, "What's happening to me?" You might wonder why you're feeling stressed, emotional, or restless. Reminding yourself about your worries can help you regain a sense of control, as well as help you gain self-awareness.

For instance, you may feel self-conscious about leading a meeting at work, and by looking at your action, you realize one of your worries is being overly concerned about what other people think. This realization can bring immediate peace to your situation, and you might see your worrying is what's causing you to panic, not the workload.

The brain perceives anything that's uncertain as dangerous, therefore, by listing your worries (being very specific about each one of them), you can minimize uncertainty and reduce the level of threat you feel in your environment. Every now and again, review your worries and determine whether they are still relevant. Perhaps you have overcome those fears already and celebrate yourself, or you might have new fears to add to the list which warrant reflection.

2. Make a List of Possible Solutions

It's easy for your mind to focus on the worst-case scenarios, but this won't help you manage your anxiety. Instead, include all the possible solutions you can think of in your action plan, and refer to these solutions when you're looking for advice or need to make a healthy decision. The goal here is to focus on actionable solutions that are within your control. Try not to include solutions that need a lot of money or time. Ideally, you should be able to implement these solutions on the go and feel instant relief.

If you can't think of any solutions to curb or manage your anxiety, consider the positive decisions you have made in the past to manage your anxious feelings. Did you enjoy journaling? Painting? Listening to your favorite music? If these strategies worked, add them to your list of possible solutions.

Here are some ideas to get you inspired:

- Get to bed earlier
- Go on a social media detox
- Have a catch-up call with a loved one
- Create a vision board
- Pray
- Practice positive affirmations

- Try out a new cooking recipe
- Try out a new sport
- Pamper yourself at the salon
- Distance yourself from negative people

3. Know Your Emotional Triggers

Write down as many emotional triggers that you are aware of in your action plan. Emotional triggers almost always have roots in the past and come as a result of unresolved feelings about particular past events. Some emotional triggers are easily detectable because you are familiar with how they manifest and where they come from. However, there will be some emotional triggers you cannot easily trace. For example, a random panic attack at night can leave you wondering where it came from or which thought induced it.

In cases like these, it's important to identify patterns and let them lead you on a trail. You may have had a panic attack after thinking about your troubled relationship with a loved one, and this particular relationship is stressful because you have unresolved feelings about how it has unfolded over the years. When identifying your emotional triggers, you may have to play detective and follow the emotional trail until you get to the root of the trigger.

Once you have identified the emotional trigger, write down your typical reaction to it. This will help you recognize when this reaction is likely to be triggered again. For instance, not all expressions of anger or emotional outbursts are caused by emotional triggers, and it would be unfair to treat them in that manner. Sometimes you will react with anger because the situation legitimately warrants that kind of response, and other times, you will react with anger because you're emotionally triggered.

4. Conduct Your Own Strength Inventory

Overcoming anxiety requires a strong level of resilience. Resilience is what helps you withstand challenges and encourage yourself to continue moving forward. While your support system can be a significant source of strength, there will be times in life when you need to motivate yourself and bounce back from hardships. Create a strength inventory listing all of your strengths, skills, and natural gifts that you could tap into when you need encouragement. Do you have great time management skills? Are you empathetic? Do you have a positive attitude about life? If you cannot think of any strengths, reach out to close family and friends and ask them to name a few positive qualities they appreciate about you. Add these qualities to your inventory and be sure to thank those who responded for their kind words!

If you're interested in building good habits, identify the obstacles standing in your way so you can move from point A to point B effortlessly. Celebrate when you reach milestones (no matter how insignificant you think they may be). You don't have to throw a party; just do something small to treat yourself, like taking an art class you've been eyeing out or getting a relaxing massage.

Committing to your action plan is important when seeking to eliminate terrible anxiety. There will be times where you forget to pull out your plan or you resort to the unhealthy habits you've used in the past to deal with your anxiety. Don't beat yourself up about this. It takes a lot of practice to adjust behaviors, so keep practicing positive coping mechanisms, and know that better days are ahead!

CONCLUSION

Severe blows in your life can lead to you developing anxiety, and in extreme cases, depression. On the outside, you may continue life as normal, and those around you may not see the emotional whirlwind you are experiencing internally. I guess that's the dark side of mental health conditions—all the action happens in the mind where no one else can see it.

Conclusion

If you've ever felt like you were going crazy during an anxiety attack, it's probably because you were experiencing a feeling no one else around you could relate to. Does this make you crazy? Well, I don't think so, but it shows how brave you are to embrace two realities—the one inside your mind and the one happening outside of it—simultaneously.

No one usually says this, but I think having anxiety reveals hidden superpowers. Think about it for a second: When you're triggered by an emotion, your mind teleports you to the past or the future, and for a few minutes you are either reliving events or experiencing future events for the first time. It's a pity that your fears piggy-back on this time-traveling experience and cast a dark cloud over it.

Imagine if you could acknowledge and accept your fears, so that whenever your mind took you on a time-traveling trip, your experience wasn't so overwhelming. How extraordinary would that be? Reliving memories from your past or thinking about the future wouldn't be as uncomfortable as it normally is. Every person has different fears that seek to steal the joy in their lives. Some people either:

- Lose their jobs or feel betrayed and anxious about their career.
- Fear they won't be able to pay off their $30,000 student debt.
- Lose a loved one and feel incredibly alone.
- Freak out thinking they are too psychologically damaged for their significant others.

The question I have sought to answer in this book is: How do you handle the crippling fear induced by anxiety?

We all know the list of unhealthy coping mechanisms, like turning to drugs and alcohol, mixing with the wrong crowd, self-isolating for extended periods, and avoiding any kind of change. But these coping mechanisms aren't sustainable in the long run, and certainly won't help us reduce our anxiety. The truth is, to

Conclusion

address and manage our anxiety, we need to commit to doing things differently, and by this, I mean learning to acknowledge, accept, and release our powerful emotions.

Anxiety tells us to run and hide when faced with difficult emotions, but hiding doesn't address the threat. Even once our panic attack has subsided, the threat still exists for as long as we aren't willing to face it. Acknowledging how we feel isn't as intimidating as it seems. Every human being has emotions and naturally reacts to different life experiences. Our emotions aren't our enemies, but instead, they are psychological tools we can use to determine how we feel about various situations and figure out what we need to change.

In this book, I have given you 7 Explosive Steps broken down into tips, strategies, and techniques you can incorporate into your daily routine to help you manage anxiety. These aren't easy fixes, as you will probably need to practice them consistently to see amazing results. When committing to addressing your anxiety, remember that it took many years to develop, and thus, it will take several months or years for you to overcome it. Don't be discouraged when you have bad days, since having bad days are a normal part of the human experience. Simply pick yourself up and get back on track, making good decisions that lead to favorable outcomes.

If you have enjoyed reading this book, I encourage you to please leave a kind review so that it will benefit a lot more people like us. Your support is greatly appreciated!

REFERENCES

Editors of Everyday Health. (n.d.). *9 Bad eating habits and how to break them*. Everyday Health. https://www.everydayhealth.com/diet-and-nutrition-pictures/bad-eating-habits-and-how-to-break-them.aspx

ADAA. (2021). *Substance use*. Adaa.org. https://adaa.org/understanding-anxiety/co-occurring-disorders/substance-abuse

Aggarwal, A. (2016, September 20). *Failure is first attempt at learning*. Buddymantra. https://buddymantra.com/failure-first-attempt-learning/

Ahuja, A. (2020, October 26). *The power of positive repetition can change your life*. One World News. https://www.oneworldnews.com/power-of-positive-repetition/

Allen, S. (2018, May 10). *Why is gratitude so hard for some people?*

Greater Good. https://greatergood.berkeley.edu/article/item/why_is_gratitude_so_hard_for_some_people

Annie. (2018, April 18). *Sleeping with anxiety.* Mind.org.uk. https://www.mind.org.uk/information-support/your-stories/sleeping-with-anxiety/

Barr, S. (2019, January 22). *Naming your anxiety.* Donegal Woman. http://www.donegalwoman.ie/2019/01/22/naming-your-anxiety/

Battles, M. (2021, January 12). *15 Ways to practice positive self-talk for success.* Lifehack. https://www.lifehack.org/504756/self-talk-determines-your-success-15-tips

Bentley, J. (2018, May 22). *What you need to know about anxiety medication: Pros and cons.* Resources to Recover. https://www.rtor.org/2018/05/22/anxiety-medication-pros-and-cons/

References

Boss, J. (2015, March 1). *13 Habits of humble people*. Forbes. https://www.forbes.com/sites/jeffboss/2015/03/01/13-habits-of-humble-people/?sh=e3c054e49d51

Buckley, G. (2020, July 2). *Basking shark*. Biology Dictionary. https://biologydictionary.net/basking-shark/

Butler, L. (n.d.). *Developing your support system*. University at Buffalo School of Social Work. http://socialwork.buffalo.edu/resources/self-care-starter-kit/additional-self-care-resources/developing-your-support-system.html

Carington, J. (2015, May 18). *Sometimes it's okay to freak out*. Jen Carrington. http://www.jencarrington.com/blog/2015/5/16/sometimes-its-okay-to-freak-out

Centers for Disease Control and Prevention. (2020, October 1).

Drinking too much alcohol can harm your health. Learn the facts / CDC. Www.cdc.gov. https://www.cdc.gov/alcohol/fact-sheets/alcohol-use.htm#:~:text=What%20is%20excessive%20drinking%3F

Chesak, J. (2020, June 26). *Tools and tricks to calm your anxiety and actually get some sleep.* Healthline. https://www.healthline.com/health/mental-health/tools-and-tricks-to-calm-your-anxiety-and-actually-get-some-sleep

Collins, N. (2013, February 25). *Lack of sleep "switches off" genes.* The Telegraph. https://www.telegraph.co.uk/news/science/science-news/9892792/Lack-of-sleep-switches-off-genes.html

Dershowitz, S., & Hudson, L. (2021, March 8). *Anxiety stats in the U.S. The Checkup.* https://www.singlecare.com/blog/news/anxiety-statistics/

References

Editors of Leesa. (n.d.). *How electronics affect sleep and why to avoid them in bed.* Leesa Sleep. https://www.leesa.com/blogs/mattress-and-sleep/5-reasons-to-ban-electronics-from-the-bedroom

Editors of Mental Help. (2016). *Anxiety hotline number.* Mentalhelp.net; https://www.mentalhelp.net/anxiety/hotline/

Editors of Mindfulness Exercises. (2019, November 12). *Dealing with negative thoughts.* Mindfulness Exercises. https://mindfulnessexercises.com/dealing-with-negative-thoughts/

Editors of Mindfulness Exercises. (n.d.). *Relieving anxiety - Guided meditation script.* Mindfulness Exercises. https://mindfulnessexercises.com/relieving-anxiety/

Edwards, N. (2015, January 16). *What it really means to have a supportive partner*. Tiny Buddha. https://tinybuddha.com/blog/what-it-really-means-have-supportive-partner/

Elmer, J. (2018, November 14). *Smiling depression: What you need to know*. Healthline Media. https://www.healthline.com/health/smiling-depression#symptoms

Emmons, R. (2013, November 12). *What gets in the way of gratitude?* Greater Good. https://greatergood.berkeley.edu/article/item/what_stops_gratitude

Fox, M. (2018, August 22). *Why expecting perfection sets you up for failure*. Forbes. https://www.forbes.com/sites/meimeifox/2018/08/22/why-expecting-perfection-sets-you-up-for-failure/?sh=35dbf06863f2

Griffin, T. (2020, November 25). *How to learn from failure. Business.com*. https://www.business.com/articl

es/learning-from-failure/#:~:text=When%20you%20encounter%20failure%2C%20tackle

Herring, M. P. (2010). The effect of exercise training on anxiety symptoms among patients. *Archives of Internal Medicine*, *170*(4), 321. https://doi.org/10.1001/archinternmed.2009.530

Higuera, V. (2020, August 25). *8 Effective ways to fight anxiety without drugs*. Healthline. https://www.healthline.com/health/effective-ways-to-fight-anxiety-without-drugs#8.-Live-in-the-moment

Hull, M. (2020, December 24). *Anxiety triggers*. The Recovery Village. https://www.therecoveryvillage.com/mental-health/anxiety/related/anxiety-triggers/

Iliades, C. (2018, January 5). *7 Causes of Anxiety*. EverydayHealth.com.

https://www.everydayhealth.com/anxiety-pictures/7-surprising-causes-of-anxiety.aspx

Keltner, D., & Marsh, J. (2015, January 8). *How gratitude beats materialism*. Greater Good. https://greatergood.berkeley.edu/article/item/materialism_gratitude_happiness

Lim, T. (2020, December 11). *10 Clear reasons why you shouldn't care what others think*. Lifehack. https://www.lifehack.org/articles/productivity/10-clear-reasons-why-you-shouldnt-care-what-others-think.html

Liu, J., Gong, P., Gao, X., & Zhou, X. (2017). *The association between well-being and the COMT gene: Dispositional gratitude and forgiveness as mediators*. Journal of Affective Disorders, 214, 115–121. https://doi.org/10.1016/j.jad.2017.03.005

References

MacCormick, H. (2020, October 7). *How stress affects your brain and how to reverse it*. Scope. https://scopeblog.stanford.edu/2020/10/07/how-stress-affects-your-brain-and-how-to-reverse-it/

Manson, M. (2020, December 18). *The fear of the unknown*. Mark Manson. https://markmanson.net/the-fear-of-the-unknown

Michaud, E. (2019, February 13). *Why you still can't forgive yourself for something you did 10 years ago*. Prevention. https://www.prevention.com/life/g20512857/how-to-forgive-yourself-no-matter-what/

Morris, T. (2017, February 3). *Brain food*. Healthy Food Guide. https://www.healthyfood.com/advice/brain-food/

Pettit, M. (2020, July 10). *6 Ways to start developing a gratitude mindset*. Thrive Global.

https://thriveglobal.com/stories/6-ways-to-start-developing-a-gratitude-mindset/

Public Health Agency of Canada. (2020). *Mental health support: get help - Canada.ca*. Canada.ca. https://www.canada.ca/en/public-health/services/mental-health-services/mental-health-get-help.html#a1

Raven, K. (2020, May 21). *Stress, anxiety, or depression? Treatment starts with the right diagnosis*. Yale Medicine. https://www.yalemedicine.org/news/stress-anxiety-depression

Robinson, L., Segal, J., Smith, M. (2020, October). *The mental health benefits of exercise*. HelpGuide. https://www.helpguide.org/articles/healthy-living/the-mental-health-benefits-of-exercise.htm#:~:text=And%20it

Schenck, L. (2012, January 9). *How to mindfully sit with anxiety*. Mindfulness Muse.

References

https://www.mindfulnessmuse.com/mindfulness-exercises/how-to-mindfully-sit-with-anxiety

Scott, E. (2020, June 8). *For such a time as this: A plan of action for general anxiety and depression*. Counseling Today. https://ct.counseling.org/2020/06/for-such-a-time-as-this-a-plan-of-action-for-general-anxiety-and-depression/

Shrapnel, R. (2017, January 15). *Gratitude grows from humility*. Richard Shrapnel. https://richardshrapnel.com/gratitude-grows-from-humility/#:~:text=The%20ability%20to%20be%20truly

Stanborough, R. J. (2020, July 23). *Fear of the unknown: Causes, symptoms, risk factors, and treatment*. Healthline. https://www.healthline.com/health/understanding-and-overcoming-fear-of-the-unknown#about